MAKING THEIR WAY

MAKING
THEM PAY

HOW TO GET THE MOST FROM
HEALTH INSURANCE AND MANAGED CARE

Rhonda D. Orin

ST. MARTIN'S GRIFFIN NEW YORK

This book is dedicated, with love,
to my husband, my children, and my parents.

www.stmartins.com

Book design by Richard Oriolo

ISBN 0-312-26760-6

First Edition: April 2001

10 9 8 7 6 5 4 3 2 1

A NOTE TO READERS

CONTENTS

Now—Make Them Pay!

ACKNOWLEDGMENTS

Many, many people and organizations assisted in the writing of this book. Principal thanks go to Eugene R. Anderson, Esq., the founding partner of Anderson Kill & Olick and the dean of the policyholders' bar.

Invaluable assistance was provided by many people who reviewed this book in manuscript form. They include John Doyle, Michele Gallagher, Norman Gerstein, Alan Golden, Dr. Evelyn Karson, Laurie Levy-Page, Andrew Swire, and Joshua Rubins. Various organizations, including Families USA and the Kaiser Family Foundation, shared useful information about consumer issues, sometimes in person and sometimes anonymously through their Web sites. Thank you for your help.

I'm grateful to my agents, Stedman Mays and Michael Mezzo of the Clausen, Mays & Tahan Literary Agency, and also to St. Martin's Press, especially my editor, Dorsey Mills, and my longtime friend Jennifer Weis.

Finally, I'd like to thank my clients. So many of you told me, after your issues were resolved, that we should find a way to tell everyone how to hold their own against insurance companies. I hope this book is what you had in mind.

WHY I WROTE THIS BOOK, AND WHY YOU NEED TO READ IT

I think that I decided to write this book the day I received the following denial of coverage from my health insurance company:

> **This service is not eligible for reimbursement as separate procedure since it is considered part of a more global procedure and is therefore considered an inclusive procedure.**

Now, they weren't going to pay me. I figured that out. But when it came to this so-called "explanation" for their decision, I read it over and over . . . then burst out laughing.

You see, I am a lawyer, with a speciality in suing insurance companies. For more than ten years, I have helped policyholders reverse incorrect coverage denials, varying from minor medical claims to multimillion-dollar corporate disputes. I have read insurance policies until I know them by heart, cross-examined hundreds of insurance executives, and argued insurance cases all over the United States.

I also am a mother of three boys who do things like break out in high fevers at 2:00 A.M. All too often, after I spend the day battling my clients' insurance companies, I spend the evening arguing with my own.

Yet, with all that experience, I still couldn't make sense of that so-called "explanation."

At first I figured that the letter must have been a mistake. That garbled sentence must have been typed incorrectly; surely the insurance company could not have written it that way on purpose.

Then it dawned on me that there was no mistake. The insurance company had meant to send out this incomprehensible "explanation." It must have made sense to them, so maybe they didn't realize that it wouldn't make much sense to me, or anyone else. And even if they realized it, maybe they wouldn't care.

That's why I sat down to write what I loosely envisioned as a consumers' survival guide. Sure, it would teach people what to do about denials like these. But it also would teach other things that so many people need to know, like how to pick out the best health plans, how to understand what coverage they're supposed to receive, and how to make their insurers pay for it.

Everyone knows, or is starting to realize, that the health insurance and managed care system is out of whack. Health plans are supposed to pay your bills and to ease your mind when you have medical needs. Policies are supposed to be easy to understand. Denials, when they happen, are supposed to be in English. When people have complaints or questions, they are supposed to be able to contact their health plans and get some kind of result.

None of this is happening. Instead, fighting with health insurance companies has become a part-time job—one that

"Very scary, Jennifer—does anyone else have an H.M.O. horror story?"

you didn't apply for and don't want. The problems vary from minor irritants like slow payments to life-and-death issues like whether your insurance company will authorize a controversial bone marrow transplant as a treatment for cancer. If you want to know how widespread the problems are, just bring up health insurance at your next party. Everyone will have a story to tell.

It's gotten so bad that even the names of the policies don't make sense anymore. One plan, for example, boasts that it is "A Managed Fee-for-Service Plan with a Preferred Provider Organization and a Point-of-Service Product."

Whatever that means.

And, while the names are a problem, the plans themselves are even worse. They are filled with exclusions and exceptions, with loopholes and lingo, all set down in technical language that seems—at least, at first glance—much too hard to read and understand.

But it's time for all of this to change. The good news is that, with relatively little effort, you can make it happen.

Believe it or not, you don't have to be a rocket scientist to understand a health plan. All it takes is patience, concentration, and some common sense.

Even better news—it's not hard to challenge an unfair coverage denial and get it reversed. Many, many challenges are successful. As long as you take the time to make the phone calls and write the letters, the odds are in your favor.

Take, for example, the incomprehensible denial that I quoted in the first paragraph of this book. It turned out to be wrong and I got it reversed with just a few phone calls. And those phone calls were well worth the few hundred dollars that were at stake.

In order to get started, you only need to know a few things about reading policies, keeping records and getting mistakes corrected. *Making Them Pay* explains these basics in just eight easy steps.

In Step One, you will learn that a health plan is like a jigsaw puzzle. You start out with a jumble of pieces, scattered upside down, backward, and sideways. But, one by one, all the pieces eventually fit together to form a complete picture.

Whenever I do jigsaw puzzles, I take the same steps. First I dump the pieces out of the box. Next I stand up the cover, so I can see the completed puzzle. Then I turn all the pieces faceup and group them by color and pattern. After that, I start on the outside border. But I never start out with the piece in the upper-left-hand corner, then look for the piece that fits to its right, and so on.

It's the same with health plans. Every time I need to understand one, I do the same things in the same order. First, I skim the entire plan in order to find the important stuff, like the benefits, the exclusions, the limitations, the definitions, and so on. Then I study each section in isolation and, finally, I figure out how they fit together.

After you read Step One, you'll be able to do this too.

Once you find the key sections of your health plan, you'll need to understand what they say. You'll learn this in Steps Two and Three. Step Two analyzes the benefits sections of typical health plans: the places where the plans grant coverage. Step Three analyzes the exclusions sections: the ones where health plans take coverage away.

When you stop to think about it, your life is filled with contracts. You have a lease or a mortgage agreement, a car loan, a student loan. You have a contract to use a credit card, to have cable TV, to have electricity and water. You even have a contract to shop at Costco.

Most of these contracts are long, complicated documents, filled with small print and technical language. You probably don't understand them, and that's not great—but in most cases it's still okay. Generally you just pay the bills when they come due. In fact, you may make monthly mortgage payments for thirty years without ever knowing what your mortgage contract really says.

Your health plan, though, is a different story. This is one contract that you *must* understand. For starters, you will need to read it before you buy it, to make sure you're getting the coverage that you need. You may need to compare it to other health plans, which means you'll need to read and understand all of them. If you're leaving a job, you may need to make a quick and smart decision about whether to change to a new plan, or to pay premiums to continue your existing coverage under COBRA, which stands for the Consolidated Omnibus Budget Reconciliation Act. Eventually you may need to read your health plan for other reasons, like to prove that you're entitled to coverage that just was denied.

Sure, you could hire a professional, like a lawyer or a broker or an insurance consultant, every time you face one of these decisions. And, in some cases, professional help may be exactly what you need. But you may avoid the need for professional help in other cases, or at least be able to understand the advice you receive, after you finish Steps Two and Three.

Once you've learned how to read your health plan, you'll need to understand a few other things. One of them is costs, and that's what Step Four is all about. Here you will learn what a health plan *really* costs—not just what you'll pay for the premium. Many other costs are hidden deep in the fine print, like deductibles, co-payments, maximums, and so on. After reading *Making Them Pay*, you shouldn't be surprised by any hidden costs again.

Step Five is all about details. It will show you how to assess the little things, like how long you'll wait on hold if you need to talk to a live person about a problem. These "little things" can make a very big difference to your happiness or unhappiness as a member of the plan.

In Step Six, you'll learn record keeping. (Did you know that piling your records on top of the stereo is *not* the best system?) You won't be getting just an offhanded suggestion that you keep track of your health claims. Instead, Step Six will offer detailed day-to-day advice about an easy way to keep good and accessible records.

You need this advice now more than ever, since, these days, many specialists have emerged, promising to keep your records and supervise your health insurance for you—for a price. At times you may need to hire one of these specialists, especially if you are too sick to cope with the mechanics of health insurance, or if you are confronted with a particularly confusing insurance situation. But, most of the time, you should be able to save your money. Just buy some file folders and a notebook, and follow the advice in *Making Them Pay*.

A special feature of *Making Them Pay* is that it reveals what rights you have outside of your health plan. For example, surprisingly few people seem to know that each of the fifty states has passed laws requiring insurance companies to give certain benefits to their members—*no matter what the insurance pol-*

icies say. Often these mandates involve particular medical conditions, such as coverage for temporomandibular disorder (TMJ), infertility, particular tests and treatments for cancer, and so on.

Step Seven lists many of these mandates, state by state. It also tells you exactly how to use them, and how remarkably easy it often is to get the coverage that's mandated.

If all of the above fails to get you the coverage you deserve, then turn at last to Step Eight. Here you will learn about some of the things that lawyers do to get wrongful denials reversed. Obviously, this won't work all the time, and you should not hesitate to hire a lawyer whenever it's necessary. But many times it isn't.

Certainly lawyers can be invaluable at times, particularly for critically ill patients who are in desperate need of expensive medical services. In fact, *Making Them Pay* describes a number of cases where lawyers have achieved dramatic victories in favor of such patients.

Lawyers often are no solution, however, for people with less extraordinary problems. First, the principle is all wrong; people should be able to understand their insurance policies and to obtain the coverage that they need, at least in most cases, without turning to lawyers.

Second is the economics. Unless you get a special deal, lawyers are expensive. People cannot, and should not be forced to, pay legal fees just to obtain coverage for ordinary health care issues.

A third problem is timing. People usually need health care *when they need it*; medical problems do not wait on the shelf while lawyers fight with insurance companies. Horror stories abound about policyholders who sicken and suffer while fighting with their insurance companies about important health services. The topic is half national outrage and half joke, popularized in movies like *The Rainmaker* and *As Good as It Gets*.

Fourth, many health plans are protected from lawsuits through either federal law or mandatory-arbitration provisions in their standardized contracts. These laws and provisions curtail one of the best weapons in a lawyer's traditional arsenal: the threat of bringing a lawsuit.

To understand why, and to understand much about health insurance in general, I'm afraid you'll need to take a brief spin through Insurance 101. The good news is that it won't take long and that, when it is over, you probably will understand things about health care that you've heard on the news, but that never made much sense to you.

The first lesson is about a federal law written in 1974, known as ERISA. ERISA leads this particular curriculum because it happens to regulate the health insurance possessed by most people in this country.

ERISA is an incredibly complicated statute that some people nickname Every Ridiculous Idea Since Adam. What ERISA actually stands for is the Employees' Retirement Income Security Act. The name doesn't have anything to do with health insurance but, unfortunately, the substance does.

ERISA was developed to govern benefit plans that are set up by private employers for their employees. It applied only to private employers, not to employers such as federal, state, and local governments, and religious institutions. The principal focus of ERISA was financial plans, such as employee retirement plans. The overriding goal appeared to be making sure that funds set aside in these financial plans were protected from misuse by the employers, and were managed properly.

As part of protecting these financial plans, ERISA established that employee benefits provided by private employers were generally the province of the federal government rather than the individual states. Among other things, ERISA established that lawsuits about these benefits should be brought in federal court and that they could only be brought under certain relatively narrow circumstances. ERISA also set limitations on the damages that could be recovered in a successful lawsuit, including a restriction against the recovery of punitive damages.

As time passed, employers began to offer health plans to their employees as part of their benefits. As a result, these health plans fell within the regulations of ERISA. Today ERISA—including its various restrictions—applies to more than half of the insured population.

The following chart, which is based on information provided by the U.S. Department of Labor and the Employee Benefit Research Institute (EBRI), a nonprofit research foundation based in Washington, D.C., illustrates the sources of insurance for those persons in the United States who had

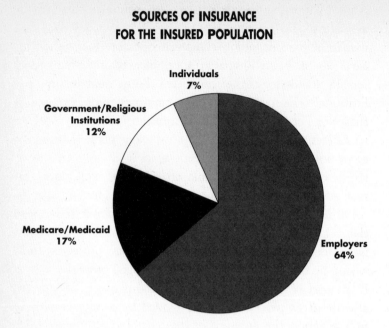

**SOURCES OF INSURANCE
FOR THE INSURED POPULATION**

Individuals
7%

Government/Religious
Institutions
12%

Medicare/Medicaid
17%

Employers
64%

health coverage in 1998. It reveals that approximately 123 million people were covered through private employers (64 percent of the insured population); approximately 33 million people were covered through public sources, such as Medicare, Medicaid, and Champus (17 percent); approximately 23 million people were covered through employment with governments or religious institutions (12 percent); and approximately 14 million people were covered through individual insurance plans (7 percent). Of the country's total population in 1998, approximately 43 million people had no insurance at all.

Stay with me for another statistic. Here it is: Not all health plans that are governed by ERISA are the same. In 1998, at least, a minority of them—no more than 45 million (37 percent)—were fully self-funded plans. While you don't need to know exactly what that means, you do need to know that such plans generally are believed to be exempt from most, if not all, state laws. This usually is interpreted to include the state mandatory-benefit laws set forth in Step Seven, and the state external-review laws set forth in Step Eight.

For the more than 60 percent of the people who got their health coverage through private employment in 1998, though, these state laws *did* apply—just as they applied to the people who got their insurance from other sources. And, while the exact numbers and percentages have varied since that time, the legal principles and limitations behind them have remained the same.

A detailed discussion of ERISA is way beyond the scope of this, or any, class in Insurance 101. All you really need to know is that, if you are one of the more than 100 million people who get your health coverage through private employment, ERISA may limit your rights to pursue lawsuits in court. If you also are in the subset of people whose private employers have fully self-funded health plans, ERISA also may limit your rights under certain state laws, such as your right to receive the protections of the state mandatory-benefit laws or of state laws requiring external review of coverage denials.

The second lesson is about government regulation of health insurance in general. In short, regulatory authority is scattered among various departments in federal and state government, and the results are very confusing. Owing to ERISA, for example, employee benefits are regulated by the U.S. Department of Labor. This means that health plans provided by private employers are regulated in large part by the Labor Department instead of, say, the Department of Health and Human Services.

In other cases, health insurance is regulated principally by the fifty states, usually through their Insurance Departments or Departments of Corporations. This is consistent with a federal statute called the McCarran-Ferguson Act, which dates back to 1945. In the McCarran-Ferguson Act, Congress decided that the insurance industry would be exempt from federal regulation—including even the federal antitrust laws. The act established that, in most cases, the responsibility to regulate the business of insurance is solely with the states.

What we have ended up with is a system where some types of health plans are regulated principally by the state governments; others are regulated principally by the federal government; and still others are regulated by both. This is very difficult for most people to understand—especially people who are simply trying to go see their doctors, get their prescriptions filled, and get their claims paid.

A lot of money has been spent in recent years trying to improve this situation. Particular attention has been paid to easing the various restrictions that ERISA places upon the rights of health care consumers. All three branches of the federal government—the executive, the legislative and the judiciary—have devoted countless hours to such problems, and the state legislatures and courts have done so as well. Periodically, changes are being made.

The third and final lesson in this curriculum is about the evolution of managed care. A number of years ago, health care costs were skyrocketing and everyone was talking about how to get them under control. Managed care was perceived as a solution that would protect consumers from excessive medical bills. Those were the days when the doctor was the "enemy" and the managed care plan the consumer's friend.

The pendulum, however, has swung in the other direction. Now the consumers, along with the doctors, the hospitals, and everyone else, are complaining bitterly about a "solution" gone wild.

All of this has led directly to the eight-step plan set forth in *Making Them Pay*.

In most cases, these eight steps should be all you need to protect your health, your sanity, your wallet—and maybe even your life. If you get in the habit of following these steps, you'll become the best kind of consumer: one who makes educated, economical choices among health plans, who understands his or her rights under these plans, and who asserts them effectively.

And, when you become this person, you'll be helping everyone else. Because an important part of helping the system to improve involves each and every one of us taking an active role toward health insurance and managed care.

Good luck, and get going. It's time to start *Making Them Pay.*

THE NUTS AND BOLTS

LOOK OVER YOUR HEALTH PLAN AND FIND THE KEY PIECES

I t's time to get down to business—and that means learning the nuts and bolts of health plans. I hate to say it, but you just can't avoid this part. Whether you are trying to pick a health plan or to figure out if something is covered under the one you've got, you need to know how to read a plan.

This chapter is about learning an *approach*—nothing more than that. The approach is one you should follow with any health plan (and, to a certain extent, with any contract at all). You should follow this approach to figure out if you're covered for anything—from open heart surgery to childhood immunizations. This is basically the same approach that a Supreme Court justice would follow, or a claims examiner at your insurance company for that matter. As far as I can tell, it's the only way to do it.

The first step is simply to find all of the important sections. *Don't* try to study them in any detail, or spend any time figuring out what they mean. At this point, just finding them is enough; you'll do the rest in Steps Two and Three.

Believe me, finding the key sections is not as easy as it seems. While all health plans contain the same basic sections—like benefits, exclusions, definitions, and so on—each plan seems to put these sections in a slightly different order and to use different titles and terms. Learning how to find them all is more than enough for Step One.

To figure out the structure of your plan, it's best to work with an example. Let's say you have allergies, and you want to know if they're covered under your health plan. Let's say that your health plan is the composite one that's set forth in Appendix A.

By the way, I created this composite, rather than using an actual plan as an example, because I wanted to show that this approach works for all plans, not just for a particular one. This composite is an HMO plan with a Point-of-Service option, meaning the right to see doctors outside the plan, and to submit the bills for reimbursement the old-fashioned way. Its text, and its basic format, is drawn from a number of actual plans.

This composite may seem much more detailed than the materials you've been given about your own plan. Sometimes people have nothing more in their files than one- or two-page summaries of their benefits, usually in a column format. If that's all you have, you're entitled to much more information—and you definitely will need it in order to understand your coverage. Accordingly, it would be a good idea for you to contact your employer or your insurance company and ask for a copy of the entire contract and/or a short version known as the Summary Plan Description or SPD.

By now you know that your first step is just to locate all the important sections, starting with the Benefits. You also know that you're learning an approach—you're certainly not learning whether or not a particular condition actually is covered under a particular health plan.

In fact, if you want to do a quick test of your insurance knowledge, turn to the composite plan in Appendix A right now and see if you can identify all of the sections that relate to allergies. Then, return to this chapter and see if there were any that you missed.

For everyone else, let's get started.

1. THE BENEFITS

It's pretty easy to find the Benefits section in your health plan. It starts at the end of the plan's seventh page. (Remember what I said in the Introduction about not starting on page 1?) In fact, you'll find five entirely different Benefits sections. They are labeled as (1) Medical and Surgical Benefits; (2) Hospital/Extended Care Benefits; (3) Emergency Benefits; (4) Mental Conditions/Substance Abuse Benefits; and (5) Prescription Drug Benefits.

Before we're done, I'll end up suggesting that you skim through all five of these sections. For starters, though, you should focus on the Medical and Surgical Benefits subsection. When you turn to it, you'll find a page that looks like this:

---

1. MEDICAL AND SURGICAL BENEFITS

A. What Is Covered

A comprehensive range of preventive, diagnostic, and treatment services is provided by Plan doctors and other Plan providers. This includes all necessary office visits; you pay a $5 office visit co-pay, but no additional co-pay for laboratory tests, X rays, and prenatal office visits. You pay nothing for well-child care for children under five years of age. Within the service area, house calls will be provided if in the judgment of the Plan doctor such care is necessary and appropriate; you pay nothing for a doctor's house call, or home visits by nurses and health aides.

(continued)

The following services are included and are subject to the office visit co-pay unless stated otherwise.

- Preventive care, including well-baby care and periodic check-ups (co-pay waived for well-child care for children under age five)
- Voluntary sterilization and family planning services
- Diagnosis and treatment of diseases of the eye
- *Allergy testing and treatment, including testing and treatment materials (such as allergy serum). You pay nothing.* [Emphasis added.]
- The insertion of internal prosthetic devices, such as pacemakers and artificial joints
- Cornea, heart, heart-lung, kidney, liver, lung (single and double), pancreas and pancreas-kidney transplants; allogeneic (donor) bone marrow transplants; autologous bone marrow transplants (autologous stem cell and peripheral stem cell support) for the following conditions: acute lymphocytic or nonlymphocytic leukemia, advanced Hodgkin's lymphoma, advanced non-Hodgkin's lymphoma, advanced neuroblastoma, breast cancer, multiple myeloma, epithelial ovarian cancer, and testicular, mediastinal, retroperitoneal, and ovarian germ cell tumors. Transplants are covered when approved by the Plan Medical Director. Related medical and hospital expenses of the donor are covered when the recipient is covered by this Plan.
- Women who undergo mastectomies may, at their option, have this procedure performed on an inpatient basis and remain in the hospital up to forty-eight hours after the procedure.
- Dialysis; you pay nothing
- Chemotherapy and radiation therapy; you pay nothing
- Inhalation therapy
- Surgical treatment of morbid obesity
- Orthopedic devices, such as braces; foot orthotics, including replacement or adjustment limited to that necessitated by the member's physical changes or growth

The section continues, and you should skim the whole thing, but you've already found what you were looking for in the highlighted section: "Allergy testing and treatment, including testing and treatment materials (such as allergy serum). You pay nothing."

In isolation, it sounds great, but nothing in an insurance policy is in isolation. So turn back to the introduction to this list of benefits and read it again—very slowly and very carefully.

Sure enough, you bump right into a hidden qualification. Before you continue reading, see if you can find it for yourself. Here are the key sentences:

A. What Is Covered

A comprehensive range of preventive, diagnostic, and treatment services is provided by Plan doctors and other Plan providers. This includes all necessary office visits; you pay a $5 office visit co-pay, but no additional co-pay, for laboratory tests, X rays and prenatal office visits. You pay nothing for well-child care for children under five years of age. Within the service area, house calls will be provided if in the judgment of the Plan doctor such care is necessary and appropriate; you pay nothing for a doctor's house call, or home visits by nurses and health aides.

If you pointed to "all necessary office visits," you win the prize. This is a major hole. It basically means that someone has to decide your office visits were "necessary" for there to be coverage. And that person—whoever it is—might not see eye to eye with you (or even with your doctor) about what exactly is "necessary."

But for now, let's say you hit the jackpot. Your primary care doctor decides you have allergies that require treatment. So he or she refers you to an allergist and you start treatment, right?

Not so fast. All you get, at this point, is one or two visits with an allergist. If you want to stay within the HMO and avoid paying for a percentage of the visits yourself, the basic plan is for your primary care physician to stay in charge of your care. And—this is the deal whether or not your primary care physician knows boo about allergies.

The words that set this limitation are hidden away in my favorite section, the innocent-sounding one called Facts About This Plan:

3. Referrals for Specialty Care

Except in a medical emergency, or when a primary care doctor has designated another doctor to see patients or when you choose to use the POS benefits, to receive standard HMO benefits you must contact your primary care doctor for a referral before seeing any other doctor or obtaining special services. Referral to a participating specialist is given at the primary care doctor's discretion; if specialists or consultants are required beyond those participating in the Plan, the primary care doctor will make arrangements for appropriate referrals.

When you receive a referral from your primary care doctor, you must return to the primary care doctor after the consultation unless your doctor authorizes additional visits. For standard HMO referrals, all follow-up care must be provided or arranged by the primary care doctor. On referrals, the primary care doctor will give specific instructions to the consultant as to when services are authorized. If additional services or visits are suggested by the consultant, you must first check with your primary care doctor. Do not go to the specialist unless your primary care doctor has arranged for and the Plan has issued an authorization for the referral in advance.

If you are "lucky" enough to be really sick, though, your primary care physician has the power to turn over your care entirely to the allergist. The words that give him or her this power appear at the end of this section:

If you have a chronic, or serious medical condition that causes you to see a Plan specialist frequently, your primary care doctor will develop a treatment plan with you and your health plan that allows an adequate number of direct access visits with that specialist. The treatment plan will permit you to visit your specialist without the need to obtain further referrals.

This sounds good, but you should appreciate that behind the scenes at HMOs, various incentive structures—or penalty provisions—may keep your doctor from acting on this provision. HMOs keep records of everything done by their primary care doctors, and many of them assert liberal rights to remove doctors from their plans. So no matter how sick you are—and certainly if you're a borderline case—there are a lot of reasons why you may not be given the right to unlimited visits. (Some insight into your doctor's perspective is set forth in Step Two.)

Before moving past the Benefits section, take a minute to skim each of the other subsections. You'll need to see if there is anything specific to allergy coverage there, since there may well be. Prescription coverage, for example, can be valuable for someone with allergies, and some plans specifically refer to allergy medications in these sections. Similarly, emergency care and hospitalization can be important issues, especially for someone with a potentially acute allergic condition like severe asthma.

Your quick check should show that there are no specific provisions about allergies in these other subsections. You'll still need to look them over, as discussed in Step Two. But for now, it's time to move on to the Exclusions.

2. THE EXCLUSIONS

Exclusions are found all over health plans. Usually, they appear in the Table of Contents, under a heading called Exclusions. But they are also found in many other locations, and under many other headings. Watch out—especially when you're deciding which health plan to buy.

This particular health plan lists General Exclusions on the seventeenth page. This section is all of three inches long. If you didn't know better, you might think that this health plan doesn't have many exclusions. Boy, would you be wrong.

This is the *entire* General Exclusions section:

SECTION VI: GENERAL EXCLUSIONS

The exclusions in this section apply to all benefits. Although we may list a specific service as a benefit, we will not cover it unless your Plan doctor determines it is medically necessary to prevent, diagnose, or treat your illness or condition as discussed under Authorizations. We do not cover the following:

- Care by non-Plan doctors or hospitals except for authorized referrals or emergencies (see Emergency Benefits) or eligible self-referral services obtained under Point-of-Service Benefits;

- Expenses incurred while not covered by this Plan;

- Services that are not required according to accepted standards of medical, dental, or psychiatric practice;

- Procedures, treatments, drugs, or devices that are experimental or investigational;

- Procedures, services, drugs, and supplies related to sex transformations; and

- Procedures, services, drugs, and supplies related to abortions except when the life of the mother would be endangered if the fetus were carried to term or when the pregnancy is the result of an act of rape or incest.

You won't need to pay attention to the last three exclusions. The allergy coverage that you are looking for is not experimental, and *definitely* does not require a sex transformation or an abortion. But the first four exclusions—which are much more general—are a different story.

These exclusions make clear (sort of) that you're going to have trouble getting coverage if you see an allergist who is not on the plan. They also repeat—twice—the same "necessary" limitation that was hidden in the Medical and Surgical Benefits introduction. This limitation appears in the introduction to this section: i.e., a service that is listed as a benefit "will not be covered for you unless your Plan doctor determines it is medically necessary. . . ." It reappears in the exclusion for "Services not required according to accepted standards of medical, dental, or psychiatric practice."

Guess what? Because of this limitation, you can't be sure that the allergy coverage you're looking for is covered under this plan. There's a fatal trap in the words "according to accepted standards of medical, dental, or psychiatric practice." Words like these usually mean "according to the symptom lists that this insurance company hands out to its employees, for use in evaluating claims." Since you don't get to see these lists, you don't know what they say—and you certainly don't know whether your symptoms are enough to get you the coverage that you want.

Just for the heck of it, it would be a good idea to call up your health plan and ask for its symptom list—or whatever they call it—for allergies. Most insurance companies don't release this kind of information readily, but maybe you'll get lucky.

Having exhausted the General Exclusions section, it's time to hunt around for other exclusionary language. You won't have to look far. Each of the five Benefits subsections has a section called What Is Not Covered. You won't find these sections in the Table of Contents, and they're not called Exclusions, but they nevertheless have the power to defeat your claim for health coverage. So you better find them all.

The What Is Not Covered part of the Medical and Surgical Benefits section looks like this:

C. What Is Not Covered

- **Physical examinations that are not necessary for medical reasons, such as those required for obtaining or continuing employment or insurance, attending school or camp, or travel**
- **Dental implants**

- **Reversal of voluntary, surgically induced sterility**
- **Surgery primarily for cosmetic purposes**
- **Homemaker services**
- **Hearing aids**
- **Transplants not listed as covered**
- **Long-term rehabilitative therapy**
- **Cardiac rehabilitation**
- **Chiropractic services**
- **Organ-donor-related transportation expenses**
- **Acupuncture services**
- **Blood and blood products**
- **Treatment of obesity and weight reduction programs (except for surgery for morbid obesity)**
- **Radial keratotomy and similar surgical procedures to correct refractive error**

If you want allergy coverage, you're basically okay. There's no exclusion here that relates directly to allergies. But there could have been—and it would have been a mistake not to look.

3. LIMITATIONS, DEFINITIONS, AND THE REST

When you've finished reviewing your plan's exclusions, are you finished looking for language that can defeat coverage? Nope. Now you have to start looking for hidden exclusions— ones that call themselves limitations, definitions, and so on.

In fact, if you ever see a health plan that doesn't have many exclusions, start looking for a section with the word Limitations in it. That's probably where you'll find the usual exclusions, dressed up in other clothes.

Your health plan is no exception. The very first sentence

of the General Limitations section contains this indirect exclusion:

A. Important Notice

Although a specific service may be listed as a benefit, it will be covered for you only if, in the judgment of your Plan doctor, it is medically necessary for the prevention, diagnosis, or treatment of your illness or condition.

Here's that "medically necessary" business again. And you'll find it also in the Authorizations section:

4. Authorizations

The Plan will provide benefits for covered services only when the services are medically necessary to prevent, diagnose, or treat your illness or condition. Your primary care doctor must obtain the Plan's determination of medical necessity before you may be hospitalized, referred for specialty care, or obtain follow-up care from a specialist.

In fact, this particular version of the "medically necessary" exclusion adds something new to the mix. It makes clear that your own doctor's opinion about what is "medically necessary" is not the one that counts. What counts is what "the Plan" thinks.

"Medically necessary" appears so many ways and in so many places because medical necessity is what managed care is all about. In fact, a "medically necessary" requirement is increasingly becoming part of even the traditional, pick-your-own-doctor insurance plans. Health plans "manage care"—and thereby costs—by limiting their payments to services, procedures, treatments, and medications that are "medically necessary." The problem is that these same health plans have a financial interest in deciding that things are *not*.

Health plans typically promise that all decisions about medical necessity are based on neutral and scientific criteria, assessed by experienced personnel in a balanced fashion. But, at the same time, they typically are closemouthed about both the criteria used and the mechanics of the decision-making process. This closemouthed approach, especially when combined with their financial interest in saying no, leads to a lot of controversy.

Your next step is to look for a Definitions section, because this is a favorite place for hiding exclusions. In this particular plan, the section appears at the end. Numerous definitions in this section may have bearing upon your allergy problems, including the definitions of "Medical Emergency," "Medically Necessary," "Precertification," "Preexisting Condition," and "Reasonable and Customary." Be smart, and read them all.

When you're done skimming the entire plan for hidden exclusions, you can return to the original question: are your allergies covered? Your answer, at this point, is the same—yes, at least to some extent—as long as you can overcome the initial barriers of "medical necessity."

4. THE CONDITIONS

Conditions are different from hidden exclusions. They basically involve mistakes that *you* can make, that can keep you from getting the coverage offered by the plan. Probably the most vilified condition, which is found in many plans, is the requirement that you must call the plan for authorization before you head to an emergency room, or at least within a certain number of hours of your visit.

These conditions can be traps for the unwary. You forgot to call? You lost your coverage. You were distraught because your two-year-old daughter was deathly ill with meningitis? We understand, but it *was* your duty to call. The hospital bill is prohibitive? We're so sorry. It's too bad you forgot to call.

Conditions can be even harder to find than limitations.

The plan we're studying, for example, doesn't contain a single section called Conditions, or any variation of the term. But read the plan carefully—you'll find them.

Here's a great example of a camouflaged condition. It's back in that section called Facts About This Plan:

4. Authorizations

If you require hospitalization, your primary care doctor or authorized specialist will make the necessary arrangements and continue to supervise your care.

Get it? It's hard to see. The condition is that you can't go an emergency room unless you first get permission from one of your doctors on the plan.

Start Laughing—or You'll Start Crying

So you've decided to take charge of your health insurance problems. You've looked over your plan and found that you really can't tell whether it covers something you happen to care about. You've decided to telephone your insurer and ask for an explanation, instead of just sighing and sticking the plan back under the TV. What do you do first?

Get a cup of coffee.

I'm serious. And don't stop there. Before you dial, you should also do the following. Put together some reading material, or paperwork, or whatever you care to do. Make a trip to the bathroom. Get a pen and paper handy. Take care of anything that absolutely must get done in the next half hour or so, like picking up children at school, or calling your staff.

The point is that the phone call is going to annoy you. It will take too long. You'll be trapped until it's over. No one will understand your questions. You may be confused, infuriated, or *enraged* by what you're told. You may, after an hour on the phone, accomplish absolutely nothing, and be told that you need to call a different department the next day.

(continued)

Because you can't do anything about these problems, you might as well fix the ones you can. Make yourself comfortable before you call. Get something productive done while you're a prisoner on hold. And don't get boxed in with other time commitments that will make you even crazier, as the minutes slip away.

And, most important of all, get your attitude in the right place. You *know* you're headed into frustration. So mellow out, accept the inevitable, and look out for the humor in the situation.

You know, I've got a lot of things to do besides call my insurance company. Like buy groceries and empty the dishwasher; like take depositions and go to court; like look over homework and play with my children; and maybe, someday, take a nap. If I thought about it, I could get quite angry about the amount of time I have to spend keeping my insurance company from keeping my money.

So—I've just decided not to think about it. Because getting angry would only make it worse. Some things have to get done, whether you like it or not. Paying taxes is one of them. So is fighting with insurance companies.

The way I see it, there are three choices. You can get angry. You can get ripped off. Or you can take on your insurance companies and make a game out of it.

I prefer the third way. Try it—you may like it too. Not only can it do incredibly important things, like save your money and get much needed health care for you and your loved ones, it also can keep you sane.

The condition is explained further in the Emergency Benefits section. There the plan gives you the option of going straight to a hospital in "extreme emergencies, if you are unable to contact your doctor. . . ." Be very careful, though. You and the plan may have different opinions about what is "extreme." You may also disagree about how hard you were supposed to try—in the middle of the crisis—to contact your primary care doctor.

This condition won't help you to figure out whether you have allergy coverage. But if you do pick this plan, knowing

*"You don't know how lucky you are! A quarter of
an inch either way, and it would have been outside
the area of reimbursable coverage!"*

about this condition can make the difference between coverage or no coverage if you ever find yourself gasping for air
during an allergy-triggered asthma attack.

5. POINT-OF-SERVICE OPTION

One more question—what do you do if your primary care
physician won't let you see an allergist as much as you like? If
you're in a straight HMO, you're out of luck, unless you have
a lot of money to spend on uncovered health care. This par-

ticular health plan, though, offers a Point-of-Service (or POS) option, which means that you can see an allergist anyway, and still get some benefits, by going off the plan.

A POS option enables you to do what the insurance industry calls "self-refer." This fancy term basically means: see a doctor who's not a part of the HMO even though your primary care physician hasn't sent you there.

To analyze a POS option, you need to review its terms the same way you did before. So turn first to its entirely separate Benefits section. Under Medical and Surgical Benefits, you'll find the following:

At your option, you can choose to self-refer for the following services instead of getting a referral from your primary care physician. You pay 20 percent of the allowed benefit after the deductible.

- **Physician office, home, or hospital visits**
- **Specialist care and consultation**
- ***Allergy testing and treatment*** **[emphasis supplied]**
- **Maternity, annual pap smears, and pelvic exams**
- **Diagnostic laboratory and X-ray tests**
- **Surgical procedures (preauthorization required)**
- **Periodic physical exams, immunizations, and well-child care**
- **Physical, speech, or occupational therapy**
- **Home health care (preauthorization required)**
- **Durable medical equipment, prosthetics, and orthopedic devices (preauthorization required)**
- **Hearing and vision exams**
- **Family planning and sterilization**
- **Dialysis, chemotherapy, radiation therapy, and inhalation therapy**
- **Infertility services (preauthorization required)**

You found what you were looking for in the highlighted third line: "Allergy testing and treatment." But you know now to keep looking for hidden problems. First, you note the absence of the following words that happen to be found in the HMO part of the plan: "including testing and treatment materials (such as allergy serum)." Since you now know that words in a health plan usually are not missing by accident, you make a mental note that if you go to an allergist off the plan, you may have a hard time getting these materials covered.

Next you check the section called What Is Not Eligible for Self-Referral and find nothing of any consequence. Then you skim the other Benefits sections, just to be safe, and discover— as you might have expected—another potential limitation on allergy medicine:

6. Other Covered Benefits

Prescriptions written as a result of a self-referral to a doctor are eligible for a $5 co-payment for a thirty-four-day supply as long as they are filled at a Plan participating pharmacy. If a nonparticipating pharmacy is used, you pay 20 percent of the allowed benefit after the deductible, and any cost in excess of the allowed benefit.

That's good to know. And you know to keep looking for more. So you search for exclusions, conditions, and limitations, but curiously find none in the two-page POS section. Do you conclude that there are none? No way! Instead you start searching the small print that introduces the section, looking for these limitations and perhaps others.

You'll find something important in the last paragraph of the section headed Facts About the Point-of-Service Benefits. That paragraph states:

Benefits under the Self-Referral Program *are subject to the definitions, limitations, and exclusions shown elsewhere in this brochure.* The Plan determines the medical necessity of services and supplies provided to prevent, diagnose, or treat an illness or condition [emphasis supplied].

Now you know that you're in the same position outside the plan that you were in the plan with regard to these limitations.

And, if you read the small print carefully, you know something else as well.

The second to last paragraph of this same section—the one just before the paragraph quoted above—contains another critical, but hard-to-see, limitation about out-of-network benefits. It threatens to dominate your finances and *severely* restrict the out-of-network benefits that you think you're about to receive.

Here's the paragraph:

An allowed benefit is the acceptable charge that the Plan uses to calculate the reimbursement to a health care provider that is not under contract with the Plan. The member is responsible for any amount that exceeds the allowed benefits determined by the Plan, plus the stated coinsurance payment.

Standing alone, this paragraph looks innocuous. It doesn't even look like a restriction on coverage. But it is—a big one.

This definition relates directly to all of the benefits sections in this self-referral program, with the exception of the Emergency Benefits. (That's because this plan does not offer Emergency Benefits on a self-referral basis.) Each of these sections state that you must pay 20 percent of the allowed benefit, and implies that the plan will pay the other 80 percent.

On a first reading it may look to a layman as if the plan will pay 80 percent of what he or she is billed by an out-of-network doctor. Not so. The plan will only pay 80 percent of what the plan decides is an "acceptable charge" for the service. That, of course, is after the patient pays the deductible.

And what does the plan think is an "acceptable charge" for out-of-network allergy treatments? This seems to be a state secret, never to be released to anyone—and certainly not to policyholders who will be asked to pay the difference. This "acceptable charge" concept takes many forms in insurance industry lingo. Perhaps the favorite for insurance companies—

and the most irritating for policyholders—is the generic, meaningless "usual and customary charges" or UCR. "Reasonable and customary charges" is another popular term.

You can and should do your best to discover what charges your plan deems "acceptable" *before* you visit an off-the-plan allergist and start a course of treatment. Otherwise you will not know what the plan will pay until after you undergo the treatment, submit the bills, and have large chunks of them mysteriously rejected, based on unexplained pronouncements of what is "acceptable."

6. TYPE OF PLAN

There are certain basic distinctions among health plans. The most important one probably is the source of the plan. If you went out and bought the plan for yourself, you probably have an "individual" plan. If you got the plan through your employment, you probably have a "group" plan, which may be distinguished further by designations based on the size of the group, such as Small Group Plan. If you work for the federal government, you probably have a special type of group plan: one that is part of the Federal Employees Health Benefits Program, also known as FEHBP. If you're a senior citizen, the source of at least one of your plans is Medicare, which is part of Social Security. You also may have a private plan that is designed to fill the gap of whatever Medicare does not cover, commonly known as Medigap coverage.

Even if you don't know what the labels mean, underline them or write them down on a separate sheet of paper. They are very, very important. As discussed in the Introduction, these labels may clue you in to which state and federal laws apply to the plan. While you don't need to understand all of the technical distinctions among these labels, people in the insurance industry do—and you may periodically be asked what type of policy you have. It's nice, at the very least, to be able to give the right answer.

While you're at it, pay attention to other labels that identify your plan. See, for example, if there are any limiting labels, like "hospital and surgical only." See if your health plan describes itself as "accident only." Sometimes the coverage offered by an entire plan is colored by a relatively inconspicuous label. Don't let the label be too inconspicuous for you.

HOW IT ALL FITS TOGETHER

There you have it—the basic approach you should follow in reading any health plan. The good news is that it's not really very hard; anyone can master any insurance plan if they tackle it systematically and patiently. In fact, someone who does may even know the plan better than the customer service representatives that he or she calls with complaints. And that knowledge should make all the difference when it comes to getting problems solved.

THE HEART OF ANY PLAN IS THE BENEFITS SECTION: HERE'S WHAT TO LOOK FOR WHEN YOU READ IT

N ow you know two things. One, you're supposed to read the Benefits section of a health plan first—no matter what page it's on. Two, you know how to find it.

What you don't know, yet, is how to figure out what it says. That's what this step is going to tell you.

The heart of any health plan is its Benefits section. This section is where the plan tells you the basic services that it will provide.

Benefits sections are given many different names. Some plans use the term Benefits; others call it Covered Services; still others go with What We Pay. Don't be distracted by the section headings; just look for the substance. With profound apologies to Gertrude Stein, a Benefits section is a Benefits section is a Benefits section.

In the course of researching this book, I've studied somewhere between fifty and one hundred health plans of all shapes and sizes. Certain common threads were pretty easy to see. For example, many health plans seem to provide some or all of the following types of benefits: (1) Medical Benefits; (2) Surgical Benefits; (3) Hospital Benefits; (4) Emergency Benefits; (5) Mental Condition and/or Substance-Abuse Benefits; and (6) Prescription Drug Benefits. Not every plan gives each of these areas a separate section heading, of course, but nevertheless the benefits may be in there somewhere.

To get a handle on the type of plan you have, or on one you're thinking of buying, it's a good idea to look for each of these six benefits. An orderly way to proceed is to make a chart with six columns, one for each type. If you are comparing several plans, list them down the left-hand margin. If you're just analyzing your own plan, that won't be necessary.

It's a good idea, also, to set aside a sheet of paper for questions. As you do your analysis, keep a running list of questions. When you're done, call your health plan, or any health plan you're considering, and try to review all of your questions in one sitting.

Incidentally, many plans offer a one-page summary of their benefits, either at the front or the back. That is *not* a substitute for the one I'm suggesting you make. The one I'm suggesting will set forth your opinions about the coverage and expose the important limitations that you discover. The one the plans provide usually is a sales-type document that tends to make everything sound as good as possible.

By the way, I'm suggesting this chart because people always ask me how to figure out which of several plans is best for them. This chart—while not the only way—visually helps to figure it out. But if you're feeling that this is too much work, and you know that you're not going to do it, then modify the approach until it works for you. Any systematic approach for comparing health plans should be helpful. The only thing to avoid is throwing up your hands, gambling that all plans are the same, and choosing blindly.

1. MEDICAL BENEFITS

Medical benefits are the most basic part of any health plan. With any luck you won't have a catastrophic illness or be rushed to the hospital during the year. But you certainly may go to a doctor for a checkup or the flu. When you do, this is the section that counts.

Because the Medical Benefits are the most basic of the benefits sections offered by health plans, you will need more detail about them than the others. Don't expect them to fit onto the one-page chart you're preparing. Instead, in the Medical Benefits column, just write: "See attached chart." Then make a chart on a separate page with the following columns:

Doctor Visits	Preventive Care	Diagnostic Tests	Misc. Therapy	Other Care	Other Services

If you are comparing several plans, leave plenty of space between their names; you'll find you need the room.

The first thing to look for in a Medical Benefits section is what happens with doctor visits. All benefits sections should cover various types of visits with physicians. Start out your analysis of every health plan by finding these provisions.

Just finding these provisions can be a learning experience. Health plans can say the simplest things in very different ways. Here are a few examples, varying from the simple to the obscure:

PLAN NO. 1

After the $250 calendar year deductible has been met, the Plan pays 80 percent of reasonable and customary charges for the following:
- Doctors' visits (in-hospital, home, office, and consultations)

(continued)

PLAN No. 2

WHAT IS COVERED

A comprehensive range of preventive, diagnostic, and treatment services is provided by Plan doctors and other Plan providers. This includes all necessary office visits; you pay a $5 office visit co-pay, but no additional co-pay for laboratory tests, X rays, and prenatal office visits. You pay nothing for well-child care for children under five years of age. Within the service area, house calls will be provided if in the judgment of the Plan doctor such care is necessary and appropriate; you pay nothing for a doctor's house call, or home visits by nurses and health aides.

PLAN No. 3

HOME AND OFFICE VISITS

When you use Preferred physicians, home and office visits, physicians' outpatient consultations, and second surgical opinions are paid in full under High and Standard Options after a $12 co-payment for each outpatient office visits charged. These services are paid as described above [*referring to a three-column chart*] when rendered by Participating and Nonparticipating physicians.

A good plan will make clear that second opinions are covered. If you do not find this provision, make a note to ask about it. Be wary of any health plan that does not cover second opinions; it may be a sign of chintziness that may carry into other areas.

Once you have figured out what coverage is provided for doctor visits, note the answer down in the first column of your Medical Benefits chart. A simple system, like "Office," "House," and "Second" would be fine. If you love detail, then note the payment terms, as in "Office—$5." But watch out for information overload; there's an awful lot of potential data here.

Keep alert for exclusions that may limit your right to coverage for doctor's visits, and note them down too. Exclusions will be discussed in more detail in Step Three. For now, though, you should appreciate that the first two examples set forth above contain some hidden exclusions.

The first plan, for example, limits coverage to "reasonable and customary" charges. This means that the plan will not reimburse you for any charges that the plan does not think are "reasonable and customary." The problem is that your plan probably will not tell you, before you incur the charge, what it thinks *is* "reasonable and customary." Also, you will get stuck paying the difference, if any, between this number and whatever your doctor actually charges. (A detailed discussion of this issue is set forth in Step Four.)

Similarly, the second plan limits coverage to doctor visits that are "necessary." "Necessary" is a murky term, just like "reasonable and customary." If you're catching on, you'll know by now that your health plan—not you and not your doctor—gets to decide what is and isn't "necessary." That means your health plan also gets to decide when you do and don't get paid. (This all-important term is discussed in more detail in Step Three.)

The third example does not have any hidden exclusions—at least none that are easy to find. That does not mean that such exclusions are not hidden somewhere else in the plan. In fact, not finding an exclusion in one place is usually a clue that you need to look harder elsewhere.

Your next step in reviewing the Medical Benefits section is to look at the coverage provided for preventive care. For adults, this may mean things like periodic checkups, immunizations, breast cancer screening (mammograms) for women, and cervical cancer screening (Pap smears) for women. It may also mean prostate cancer screening (PSA tests) for men.

Pay careful attention to how health plans explain their preventive care. For example, some plans list exactly which immunizations and boosters are covered, while others just promise to cover "routine immunizations and boosters" without revealing which ones. This is one way they may get you—after all, you will have no idea what the plan actually covers, but you may think you do.

You can be sure that the plans with nonspecific language maintain internal policies making clear exactly what is "routine." But you won't know what they say unless and until there is a coverage dispute. If you discover at that point that you don't like the internal policies, it will be too late to do much about it. So if you really need to know what preventive care is covered, add specific questions to your question list before you sign up. And make sure you get the answers.

Unless you are particularly interested in certain types of preventive care, all you need to note on the chart is whether the care offered is specific or vague. Whatever you do, don't write down a simple "yes" in this column for a plan that's vague. You could fool yourself into making a poor decision.

If you have children or hope to soon, you should review separately, and make a separate note in the chart about, preventive care for children. Plans vary widely in this area. What most people want is a plan that covers "well-child" visits until at least age twelve. Lots of plans do so, while some cut off this coverage as young as age two.

It's the same drill with diagnostic procedures, such as X rays and laboratory tests. Many plans make clear that such procedures are covered, but they vary dramatically in how much coverage will be specified. Some plans spell out exactly what they cover, delineating X rays, MRIs, laboratory and pathology services, and machine diagnostic tests. Others just promise vaguely to cover "necessary diagnostic procedures, such as laboratory tests and X rays." By now you know that you don't know what that *really* means.

The Chilling Disclosures of
of an HMO Medical Director

One day, Dr. Linda Peeno caused the death of a man. At least, that's what she thinks, and that's what she's told many people, including the California General Assembly and the U.S. House of Representatives.

On that fateful day, Dr. Peeno was working as a case reviewer for a managed care organization in Louisville, Kentucky. Suddenly this stranger's case file appeared in her in-box. He needed a heart transplant and he needed it soon—and the cost was estimated at half a million dollars.

"A lot of people were scurrying around trying to figure out what to do," Dr. Peeno testified before the California State Assembly in 1997. The goal, she said, was to find a way to deny the claim.

Dr. Peeno did the job; she discovered a restriction in the man's coverage that justified a denial. Then she denied the claim.

To her office, Dr. Peeno recalled, the discovery was a source of "jubilation." To the patient, it was a death sentence. To Dr. Peeno, it was a step toward the end of her career in managed care.

"Once I stamped 'Denial' on that man's form," Dr. Peeno told the California State Assembly in 1997, "his life's end was as certain as if I had pulled a plug on his ventilator. And if I knew his name, it was only for a fleeting second. I remember the details only because of the accolades it brought me from my employer."

This patient was not Dr. Peeno's only victim, she admitted to the California State Assembly with remorse. "Eventually, I made many more decisions, some of which I am equally certain caused additional pain, suffering and even death for other patients—hardly the work, I believe, of a physician."

In 1991, Dr. Peeno left the industry. She became what she calls "an advocate for ethical managed care." She insists that she is not anti-managed care, as she may be simplistically labeled. To the contrary,

(continued)

29

she originally entered the field due to her belief in the value of a managed care system.

Dr. Peeno currently chairs the ethics committee at the University of Louisville Hospital. She has provided testimony about her experiences in managed care to the U.S. House of Representatives Subcommittee on Health and the Environment, as well as many other organizations and courts.

When Dr. Peeno testified before Congress in 1997, she explained how managed care organizations profit from complicated contracts, hidden costs, confusing appeals procedures, apathetic members, and various other issues addressed in *Making Them Pay*. The following is an excerpt from her testimony:

I am a witness to the rapid growth of a monstrous business whose economic success is based upon the micromanagement of medicine through avoidance, denial and control.

How does this happen? Let's imagine that you are starting a new managed care organization and you have hired me to help you put it together. What do we do?

First, I exchange my traditional doctor's bag for a health executive's box of tricks. Second we agree that we do not want just any group of patients. We will use all the sophistication of modern advertising and marketing to ensure that we avoid those persons who cost money. We have many ways to eliminate the old, the sick, the disabled, the malignant, the chronic, the risky lifestyles, and any other who may be a drain on our premium pool.

Presuming we get a pool of healthy, prepaid members, what do we do now to ensure our maximum economic return—i.e., that we succeed in our business of health management?

First: we *limit the network*. We justify this based on costs and business necessity. It will be of no concern to us that we may create something that requires parents to travel forty-two miles in the middle of the night with a sick child.

Second: we *limit benefits, make exclusions* and *create ambiguous language* to give us the maximum power to deny services based on coverage issues. It will not worry us that we may eventually cause the death of some persons when they are told that they do not have coverage for necessary treatments. We are doing business, not welfare.

Third: we create *complex, inexplicable rules and procedures* for navigating our managed care maze. This will be some of the simplest, least questionable "denials," because we can just refer to our requirements for payment. We make the rules.

Fourth: we have our most versatile, authoritative, and profitable tool—our ability to make *medical necessity determinations.* Empowered with physicians employed by us, we become the final medical authority. Regardless of what any treating physician may want to do, we assume control and practice medicine our way.

Fifth: we cannot do everything directly, so we ensure *that our physicians* become our agents. We create *financial arrangements* that will encourage them to limit or deny directly without our intervention.

Sixth: we supplement this with extensive contracts devised to control physician's power and authority. We *profile them economically;* we lure them with *selection* and threaten *deselection* once hooked; we usurp their power and authority with *contracts full of clauses extracting performance, compliance, gag conditions, confidentiality, good managed care behavior.* We make them our agents of denial.

Seventh: For good measure, we add a *termination-without-cause* clause to give us the ultimate power of ridding ourselves of inappropriate physicians.

Eighth: Should anyone challenge our decisions, we ensure that *the grievance and appeal process* is closed and weighted against the member and in our favor.

Ninth: We add *mandatory arbitration,* in which there is no record of issue or outcome, giving no benefit to other members, case law, or public/legislative action.

(continued)

> **Tenth:** Even if all this fails, and someone should suffer from our tactics, nearly everything we do will be *shielded from any liability* thanks to our ERISA *preemption.*
>
> Finally, we work to *change medical education,* creating from the beginning manageable doctors to suit our purposes. Also, by not paying for things, and excluding everything we can under the designation of "investigational" we can *diminish research,* and slowly eliminate the availability of new treatments, prolonging of life, and added expense of the care of persons.
>
> Now—this is what is left . . . and if we work smart, we will think of ways to deny this as well. Then we will have achieved the ideal health care business: money coming in and none going out—a "medical loss ratio" of *zero.*

Write down on your question page to find out exactly what's covered, especially tests that you think may be important to you. Otherwise just fill in this column in your chart, preferably by identifying the tests actually covered or by identifying the plan as "vague."

The next issue is therapy. Most plans cover three different types as Medical Benefits: speech, physical, and occupational.

Beware of the speech, physical, and occupational therapy that is offered by many plans. Typically, this coverage is extremely limited, both in terms of *when* therapy is deemed appropriate and *how much* is deemed necessary. For example, many plans limit speech therapy to speech impairments of "organic origin." This basically means that the impairment must relate to a physical problem. In such plans, developmental problems often aren't covered (which may incline some plans toward deciding that the origin of a particular problem is developmental, rather than organic).

Many plans also limit the amount of speech therapy that they'll cover. A typical limitation is a sixty-day time period (i.e., as many times a week as a doctor will authorize—often no more than two—within sixty consecutive days). Finally, they typically cover speech therapy only if it is likely to result in a "significant improvement" in the patient's condition within those sixty days. Added together, such limitations can undercut the value of this benefit.

Speech and physical therapy can be very important, especially if you have young children. So be very careful when you review health plans in this area, and note down major restrictions in the "Therapy" column.

The "Other Care" column covers issues like dental care, vision care, home health care, infertility care, and cosmetic surgery. Many Benefits sections provide some, but very limited, coverage in these areas. For example, while they do not cover routine dental procedures and services, such as annual office visits to dentists or filling cavities, they may cover dental needs that arise out of certain types of injuries; surgery for congenital defects, such as cleft lip and cleft palate; or medical treatment for fractures, tumors, and cysts. Note in your chart whether any dental care is included, whether the coverage provisions are specific, and whether the coverage seems acceptable.

Be careful not to confuse the dental care mentioned in the Benefits section with dental care that may be offered as an option, for an additional charge.

The situation for eye care is comparable. Relatively few health plans seem to cover routine visits to eye doctors or basic eye care needs, like eyeglasses or contact lenses. Eye care under most medical plans instead is limited to the treatment of eye diseases. Still, some plans are more generous than others. For example, some of them provide broader coverage for the "diagnosis and treatment of diseases of the eye" without limitation by disease or age group. Others, in contrast, limit eye care to "nonsurgical treatment for amblyopia and strabismus, for children from birth through age twelve." Again, mark down on the chart the coverage that interests you.

Most plans cover home health care by nurses and/or aides,

when prescribed by a doctor. Many, however, do not offer extensive details about when they will provide this coverage. If you think this benefit may be important to you, ask for more information. Otherwise just review what's there and mark it down on the chart.

Limited coverage for infertility treatments is available under most plans. While most plans claim to cover the "diagnosis and treatment of infertility," the only covered treatment often is limited to intracervical insemination—and not all plans cover that. It is not uncommon to find that all assisted reproductive technology (ART) procedures are excluded, and such as intrauterine insemination (IUI), in vitro fertilization and embryo transfer.

The final column on your chart is for "Other Services." This column refers to covered services other than actual care. For example, many health plans provide coverage for oxygen, prosthetics, and durable medical equipment such as wheelchairs, crutches, and hospital beds. They may provide limited coverage for medical foods for people (sometimes just children) with inherited metabolic diseases. Some health plans provide coverage for orthotics, while others do not. Finally, most health plans provide no coverage for vision and hearing assistance, like eyeglasses, contact lenses, and hearing aids.

Review these areas, or at least the ones that are important to you, and make appropriate notes in this column of your chart.

2. SURGICAL BENEFITS

Many health plans seem to offer pretty much the same benefits for surgeries. Typical benefits seem to include at least the following:

1. transplants for the cornea, heart, kidney, lung, liver, and pancreas

2. mastectomy surgery on an inpatient basis, with a mandatory forty-eight-hour hospital stay following surgery

3. reconstructive surgery under certain conditions, including reconstruction of a breast following mastectomy

4. limited oral and maxillofacial surgery

5. voluntary sterilization

Many of them go on to offer other benefits as well, such as allogeneic and autologous bone marrow and stem cell transplants for certain specified diseases. All this list does is identify the benefits that seem to be particularly common.

Conversely, it seems pretty common for health plans to exclude things like:

1. most types of cosmetic surgery

2. radial keratotomy

3. surgery to achieve a sex transformation

4. reversal of surgical sterilization

5. certain specified transplants

In every case, you should read the words of the relevant benefit, and the relevant exclusion, very carefully. For example, while most health plans exclude cosmetic surgery, many of them leave some wiggle room in the wording of the exclusion. A typical exclusion prohibits surgery "primarily for cosmetic purposes." The key word here is "primarily." Certain types of cosmetic surgery, such as breast reductions, may be "primarily" for health reasons, yet have ancillary cosmetic benefits. Cosmetic surgery of this type should be covered despite this exclusion.

Other exclusions actually make clear that certain types of cosmetic surgery are covered. For example, one plan excludes

"[C]osmetic surgery unless required for a congenital anomaly or to restore or correct a part of the body which has been altered as a result of accidental injury, disease, or surgery." This exclusion plainly means that cosmetic surgery *is* covered when it is "required for a congenital anomaly" and in the other specified circumstances.

Unless you're dealing with a very unusual plan, it shouldn't be necessary for you to fill in much information in the "Surgical Benefits" column of your chart. Just do a quick check to make sure that all of the plans you're studying offer this standard coverage, then write "Standard" in the right spot. If one of them doesn't, write the word "Limited" or "Extra" instead. Of course, if you have a special interest in a particular benefit, you should check for this benefit in every plan you're considering and note your findings on your list.

One big difference that you may find in comparing Surgical Benefits sections is the level of detail in the plans. Some plans describe the exact benefits that members are entitled to receive, even including the all-too-visual reference to "cutting procedures." Others offer much less detail. Instead they simply say that you will have whatever "necessary" surgery is authorized by the plan doctors. These plans are problematic for anyone who wants to be an informed consumer.

Keep in mind, moreover, that the plan doctors are not really making these decisions on their own. Rather, they probably have been handed extremely detailed information by the plan regarding when they may authorize surgeries. It's standard practice, for example, for HMOs to create "symptom lists" and then to require that one or all of the symptoms on this list be present before a doctor can authorize surgery under the plan.

This leads to some practical advice. If you are deciding among several plans, and you anticipate a need for a particular type of surgery, try to find out what symptoms are on each plan's symptom list with regard to that surgery. It won't be easy, but it's well worth the effort. One route may be to call customer service and ask for this information. Another may be to call a doctor on the plan. (Many doctors may be uncomfortable with releasing this type of information so this route may not work much of the time.) The state insurance commissioner's office may provide a third option.

Your inquiry should not stop at whether a particular type of surgery is covered. Related issues can vary widely from one plan to another, like what percentage of the bill actually will be paid.

Serious problems can arise from the doctors' perspective if doctors disagree with the "symptom lists" or if they have many patients who have borderline symptoms. If the doctors authorize the surgeries anyway, they run the risk of not getting paid. If it happens often enough, they run the risk of getting blacklisted by their plans, and eventually terminated. Termination, in turn, can have permanent repercussions for their medical careers, since doctors are routinely asked to fill out forms stating whether they're ever been terminated by a managed care plan, and why. Just one termination can snowball into other problems.

To make matters worse, health plans may report such terminations to public authorities, potentially provoking extensive investigations into the doctors' medical practices—and perhaps worse. These investigations typically are very threatening experiences for doctors. They also are disruptive and expensive, and can do considerable damage to the doctors' reputations. Usually these investigations are supposed to be conducted in secret. It's all too easy, though, for the secret to leak through the medical profession, then trickle down to the patients, especially as the investigating agency contacts hospitals and other organizations, and possibly even patients, asking questions about certain doctors and/or requesting files.

If, on the other hand, doctors choose to follow their plans' symptom lists even in cases where they personally disagree, and end up refusing to perform surgeries that they might have otherwise performed, they face other problems—especially if their patients get sick. At the very least, the doctors run the risk of losing these particular patients; at the other extreme, they may face malpractice actions and permanent damage to their professional reputations.

These dilemmas, by the way, are not limited to surgical situations. They can come up in any type of situation involving the providing of care under a managed care plan.

3. HOSPITAL BENEFITS

Like surgical benefits, there seem to be certain basic hospital benefits in many health plans that I've seen. They include the following:

1. a semiprivate room, unless a private room is necessary to prevent contagion to others or for other, specific reasons

2. use of operating, recovery, and other treatment rooms

3. drugs and medicines

4. diagnostic X rays

5. dressings, splints, and casts

6. anesthetics and anesthesia service

7. blood and blood plasma, and its administration

8. preadmission testing

9. hospitalization for dental work only in limited circumstances

10. hospital visits and consultations by attending physicians

Many health plans seem to exclude the following, at least as part of their hospitalization benefits:

1. hospitalization that is not deemed to be medically necessary, such as certain admissions for observation and testing

2. personal comfort items, like TVs and telephones

3. private duty nurses

4. custodial or domiciliary care, such as companions who assist with bathing and eating

5. convalescent care

Again, a big difference is in the wording of the plans rather than in the particular benefits offered. Some plans spell out the details of their coverage, while others are much less informative.

Many plans rest entirely upon the plan doctor's purported "discretion" and provide broad-brush explanations of benefits, like:

The Plan provides a comprehensive range of benefits with no dollar or day limit when you are hospitalized under the care of a Plan doctor. You pay nothing. All necessary services are covered. . . .

While such an approach certainly seems comforting, it leaves much room for error. Patients have few options when services are refused. Even worse, when services are refused wrongly, patients rarely know it.

When you encounter such vague wording, it's a good idea to call your health plan and try to get more specific information. In particular, ask for all explanatory lists and materials that describe the services covered during hospital stays.

If you're successful, mark the information down on your

chart. If not, mark down "Vague" instead. At least, when you review the chart later, you won't be beguiled into a potentially false sense of security.

---

4. EMERGENCY BENEFITS

Expect your health plan to cover emergencies. If it doesn't get another health plan.

Most health plans seem to provide coverage for emergencies. Subject to their "usual and customary rates" (a term discussed in greater detail in Step Four), many of them cover 100 percent of all hospital and doctor bills. But, increasingly, plans impose lots of rules and regulations, like calling your primary care physician for permission to go to a hospital, notifying the plan within twenty-four hours of your emergency-room visit, going to a particular hospital, and paying parts of fees that the plans think are "unreasonable." You run the risk of forfeiting some of your coverage just because, during your crisis, you forgot to dot your *i*'s and cross your *t*'s.

You also may face quirky limitations. Some plans, for example, will not pay for normal full-term deliveries of babies outside of the service area. Some do so by stating quietly, in the Definitions section: "A near-term delivery is not a Medical Emergency." If pregnant women on this plan travel outside of the service area in the ninth month, they are taking their chances.

The best plans have relatively flexible rules regarding when to notify your health plan about an emergency. It may be a good sign, for example, when a plan requires notification as long as forty-eight hours after seeking emergency care, and does not mandate preapproval for telephone calls to 911. Other plans are rigid regarding both notification and authorization; some even refuse to pay for any emergency care that was not authorized in advance by a primary care physician.

Another issue regarding emergency care is deciding what is

an emergency. Every cough, for example, may seem like an emergency to the parents of a newborn baby—but their plans are likely to disagree. The best plans place a little trust in their policyholders and state that emergency coverage will apply if the policyholder reasonably thinks the situation is an emergency (emphasis on "reasonably"). The worst ones do the opposite; they leave you feeling afraid to decide for yourself that anything is an emergency.

In addition, if you belong to a managed care network and are treated in an out-of-network hospital, you may find yourself saddled with a big bill from that hospital even after your plan supposedly has paid. The problem is that your contract may obligate your plan to pay an out-of-network hospital only the preset fees that it would pay to a network hospital. Those fees, though, are likely to be substantially lower than the hospital's average charges.

Here's the problem. Because the hospital has no contract

with the plan, the hospital has no obligation whatsoever to accept these reduced fees. The next thing you know, the hospital will be chasing you for the difference.

Some contract language makes this limitation quite clear:

> **When you receive covered services for a medical emergency or urgent care situation from a non-Network Provider, outside of the Service Area, we will limit reimbursement to the Usual and Customary Rates for those expenses incurred up to the time the Member is determined to be able to travel to a Network Provider.**

In other contracts, however, the limitation is dangerously subtle. A great example is the provision from the composite plan set forth in Appendix A:

> **The plan pays reasonable charges for emergency services to the extent the services would have been covered if received from Plan providers. You pay $25 per hospital emergency room or urgent care center visit for emergency services that are covered benefits of this Plan. If the emergency results in admission to a hospital, the co-pay is waived.**

At a first reading, it may seem as if all you'll pay for an out-of-area emergency is $25. But when you stop and reread the first sentence, that may not be the case.

If you do get a hospital bill for an astronomical sum, and you call your plan in horror, your plan may shrug you off, stating that it paid the hospital its usual rates. Your plan may know full well that those rates were not likely to be acceptable to an out-of-network hospital. But, as it probably will convey to you, that's not the plan's problem.

Spare yourself at least some of this annoyance. Read your plan, and figure out what you're getting into, *before* the crisis hits.

Another big issue is ambulance care. Often plans state that they cover ambulance services, or at least the services necessary for transportation *to* the hospital. But read your plans very carefully. Many of them contain hidden provisions that may impair your rights to ambulance coverage.

One plan states, for example, that it will cover ambulance service "only if your condition requires the use of the medical services and supplies that only a licensed ambulance can provide and the use of other means of transportation would endanger your health." It then states, "We will not cover ambulance services in any other circumstances, even if no other transportation is available."

This language is problematic, especially in marginal cases, since most people know little to nothing about: (1) exactly what medical services and supplies they'll need; and (2) exactly which of those services and supplies will be provided while they are inside the ambulance (as opposed to inside the hospital). If you suffer from a similar lack of technical knowledge and foresight, and you have a plan with problematic qualifications—and you're not sure whether an ambulance is absolutely essential—it might be a good idea to get precertification for the ambulance *before* you place that call.

5. MENTAL CONDITIONS/ SUBSTANCE-ABUSE BENEFITS

Many different health plans (although not all) provide some form of these benefits—the issue is how much.

Some plans, for example, cover a specified number of inpatient hospital days every year for mental disorders and substance abuse. They usually cover a much larger number of outpatient visits per year: sometimes twice as many. Plans often permit members to convert unused inpatient visits into outpatient visits, frequently on a 2–1 ratio.

There are certain other patterns. For example, many plans set annual maximums and lifetime caps in this area, particularly for substance abuse. It is common, for example, for a plan to set a limit like "two confinements per lifetime for treatment of alcoholism or substance abuse." It is also common for a plan to pay less and less per outpatient visit, as time goes on. In this respect, the following provision in the composite plan in Appendix A is typical:

> **Unlimited outpatient visits to Plan doctors, consultant, or other psychiatric personnel each calender year; you pay $15 per visit for visits 1 through 5; $25 per visit for visits 6 through 30; $35 per visit thereafter for the remainder of the calendar year.**

One catch is that many plans set strict preauthorization requirements for all treatment for mental disorders and substance abuse. As usual, these plan doctors are subject to an unseen set of restrictions and guidelines. It seems as though some health plans pull out all the stops in reserving extensive discretion for preauthorization. One plan, for example, agreed to pay for "short-term inpatient psychiatric care" only "[W]hen deemed Medically Necessary, clinically appropriate, and, when in the judgment of your Primary Care Physician or Plan Provider," you need it.

Another catch is that many plans have strict requirements about the background of the person providing treatment. Some plans, for example, refuse to pay for treatment provided by certain types of social worker or other counselors, and to cover care only if provided by a psychiatrist with an M.D. degree or a psychologist with a Ph.D. Sometimes plans don't even bother to explain this limitation; it's simply inherent in their provider lists, which exclude practitioners without the required background.

Once again, whenever you're dealing with a vague plan, try your best to get detailed information.

Some states, by the way, have laws that prevent health plans from refusing to pay for services provided by particular types of providers, such as social workers, nurse-midwives, chiropractors, osteopaths, and so on. If you're dealing with a provider without an M.D. and you've encountered, or anticipate, coverage issues, you probably should check your state statutes, which are listed on the Internet, or try checking with your state insurance commissioner. Often, the providers themselves know the most about the state laws governing their specialized area. But if they don't, a contact list of the insurance commissioners for the fifty states is set forth in Appendix B; or contact an attorney.

Another important issue to consider is whether the payment by your insurer is worth the risk of a confidentiality leak. Insurers typically require the treating physician to submit detailed paperwork about highly sensitive and confidential mental problems that you are suffering before they will pay any claims. They often are required to provide a diagnosis, which to a layman may seem like an embarrassing, even pejorative, label.

While you may be given all sorts of assurances about confidentiality, you still may feel squeamish about the idea of this information being available in computer banks, for all time.

For exactly this reason, many people who can afford it financially opt for paying their own claims for mental health treatment, rather than submitting them to their insurance companies. Before you rush to submit any claims, it's a good idea to give this matter some serious thought.

6. PRESCRIPTION DRUG BENEFITS

This benefit is one of the most popular and practical benefits offered by health plans. There are, however, big differences among them. These differences include the scope of the coverage, the size of the drug supply that plans will pay for in one prescription, the co-payment, the permitted pharmacies, and the maximum amounts that they will pay in a year.

Many health plans limit this benefit to the bare minimum: prescription drugs and nothing more. Some require precertification for particular prescription drugs, such as AZT for the treatment of AIDS, growth hormones, and infertility drugs. Others exclude these and other specified drugs outright, even though they require prescriptions.

Many health plans seem to exclude the following from their prescription drug benefits:

1. nonprescription drugs

2. drugs for cosmetic purposes

3. medical supplies, such as dressing and antiseptics

4. drugs for weight loss

5. drugs to enhance athletic performance

Health plans seem to vary widely about whether they cover things like contraceptive drugs; insulin for the treatment of diabetes; or drug-related paraphernalia, such as needles and syringes. Some cover these things, others don't.

Whenever you look over a health plan's prescription-drug benefits, you should pay special attention to the amount of drugs that will be paid for at a given time. For example, many plans pay only for a thirty-day supply from a local pharmacy, which forces patients who need ongoing medicines to replenish their supply every few weeks. This restriction can be a real problem for some people, such as elderly patients during winter months.

In fact, the state of Maryland found this limitation so objectionable that it passed state legislation compelling insurers to offer ninety-day supplies. To its further credit, Maryland has policed this statute; one year, it fined a health plan tens of thousands of dollars for failing to comply.

Plans with this thirty-day restriction may offer to pay for a ninety-day supply, if purchased by mail order. Mail-order pharmacies, however, can be controversial. Some people believe that they are convenient. Others, however, dislike them because they fear their prescriptions may be lost or stolen from the mail: a development that could create medical problems along with disputes with their health plans.

You also should keep an eye on co-payments whenever you review prescription-drug benefits. Some plans set a standard co-payment, such as $10 or $15 per prescription. Some pay a percentage of each prescription, with deductibles that can reach $200 per person. And some combine these two approaches, setting a low co-payment as an incentive to get patients to use mail-order services.

CONCLUSION

I know, I know, it's a little boring. So is paying your taxes, and doing your job at times, and cleaning the dinner dishes. But you've got to do these things; they're a part of life.

Same here. You've got to know how to read a health plan, or else you'll make bad decisions, waste money, and—worst of all— be deprived of health care that you may desperately need. Under the circumstances, "a little boring" is a small price to pay.

Now That You Know How Health Plans Give Coverage, Learn All the Ways That They Take It Away

Health plans are filled with secrets—things you thought you understand when you bought your policy, but discover later you didn't. It won't be easy for you to pick a good health plan, or get the coverage you paid for, unless you crack these codes.

A common trap is when health plans grant coverage in one place, then take it away someplace else. The place that grants the coverage is the first place you'd look. The place that takes it away may be one you'd never think of.

Now, everybody knows about exclusions. They're easy. If an insurer wants you to know there's no coverage, it will use an obvious exclusion.

Not everybody knows, though, that "Limitations" often are just like exclusions. And so are some Definitions. And even some Benefits.

Here's how it works. You crack a tooth at your friend's dinner party because their two-year-old dropped a tiny little Lego piece into the meat sauce, and you bit down on it while you were eating. You rush to the dentist, confident that you are protected from "Accidental Injury" for dental care. After all, your policy stated, in its Other Medical Benefits section, that it covers:

Services, supplies, or appliances for dental care to sound natural teeth (see Definitions) required as a result of, and directly related to, an accidental injury (see Definitions).

Your claim is denied. Why? Because of your policy's definition of "Accidental Injury":

Accidental Injury: An injury caused by an external force or element such as a blow or fall and which requires immediate medical attention, including animal bites and poisonings.
Dental care for accidental injury is limited to dental treatment necessary to repair sound natural teeth. *Injury to the teeth while eating is not considered an accidental injury.*

Like a wolf in sheep's clothing, this definition is like an exclusion in disguise or, at least your insurance company may treat it like one. It may block coverage for your cracked tooth, even though it's "only" a definition.

Be smart. The most innocent parts of your policy can be the most deadly. Before you select a health plan, or incur substantial medical expenses, make sure that you've checked out the fringes of your policy—like the Definitions section, the Limitations section, and any other sections with innocuous-sounding names.

1. THE EXCLUSIONS

Exclusions are always found in at least one place: a general Exclusions section, labeled something like "Exclusions" or

"What We Will Not Cover." This section is usually easy to find, and is listed separately in the Table of Contents.

Exclusions also are scattered elsewhere in health plans. A common location is the Limitations section. Also, statements that have the effect of exclusions often are hidden in unlikely locations. For example, when "Provider" is defined in the Definitions section as meaning only medical doctors, this section may have the effect of excluding coverage for other types of practitioners, such as midwives, acupuncturists, chiropractors, and social workers.

The General Exclusions sections can vary widely from one plan to another. Some of them are very short, like the following example from the composite plan in Appendix A:

- All benefits are subject to the limitations and exclusions in this brochure. Although a specific service may be listed as a benefit, it will not be covered for you unless your Plan doctor determines it is medically necessary to prevent, diagnose, or treat your illness or condition as discussed under Authorizations in Section III. The following are excluded:

- Care by non-Plan doctors or hospitals except for authorized referrals or emergencies (see Emergency Benefits) or eligible self-referral services obtained under Point-of-Service Benefits

- Expenses incurred while not covered by this Plan

- Services not required according to accepted standards of medical, dental, or psychiatric practice

- Procedures, treatments, drugs, or devices that are experimental or investigational

- Procedures, services, drugs, and supplies related to sex transformations

- Procedures, services, drugs, and supplies related to abortions except when the life of the mother would be endangered if the fetus were carried to term or when the pregnancy is the result of an act of rape or incest

Some plans, though, have Exclusions sections that are far too long to set forth here. For example, one plan that I've seen had *forty-seven* separate exclusions that filled up five pages, even though they were single-spaced.

But don't be fooled by the length of your health plan's General Exclusions section. When this section is conspicuously short, that usually means that the exclusions have been scattered—or hidden, depending upon your perspective— throughout other sections of the plan. A short Exclusions section is nothing but a signal to look elsewhere.

Remember the plan with the very short Exclusions section? It turns out that the plan has mini-exclusions sections under each and every Benefits section. For example, the Medical and Surgical Benefits section has three subsections: What Is Covered, Limited Benefits, and What Is Not Covered. The last two sections really are Exclusions sections.

In fact, if each of the Limited Benefits and What Is Not Covered subsections, from each of the Benefits sections, were to be moved into the General Exclusions section, that section probably would switch from being the shortest Exclusions section to being the longest one.

At the end of the day, many plans seem to exclude a lot of the same stuff. The relatively generic blacklist tends to include the following:

1. Comfort or convenience items, like telephones or televisions in hospitals

2. Cosmetic, plastic, or reconstructive surgery, except in particular circumstances

3. Custodial or domiciliary care

4. Dental care, except in certain circumstances

5. Elective abortions

6. Experimental or investigational procedures, treatments, drugs, or devices

7. Hearing aids and vision aids

8. Learning and behavioral disorders

9. Long-term rehabilitative therapy

10. Transportation expenses (except for local ambulance service in certain circumstances)

11. Nonprescription drugs

12. Routine household items, such as cough syrup, bandages, and humidifiers

13. Private or special duty nursing

14. Reversals of voluntary, surgically induced sterility

15. Services that are not medically necessary

16. Sex transformations

In contrast to these common exclusions, there are many exclusions that are appear in a number of different health plans. They're not routine, but neither are they unusual. A few examples are:

1. Acupuncture treatment

2. Chiropractic treatment

3. Family planning services

4. Durable medical equipment, such as wheelchairs, hospital beds, and braces

5. Diagnosis and treatment of infertility

6. All weight-control services, including surgical treatment of morbid obesity

7. Speech therapy for nonorganic reasons

By the way, this list of less-than-common exclusions may be one way of getting an idea whether the premium you're being charged is appropriate. In every health plan, there should be a relationship between the coverage provided and the premium charged. It's a personal decision whether you prefer to spend more money in return for more coverage, or whether you wish to spend less money and are willing to accept less coverage. In order to make this decision well, though, you need to study your plan choices carefully. Make sure that you don't end up paying a relatively high premium for coverage that actually is on the restrictive side.

Exclusions, by the way, can be very deceptive. This, for example, is an exclusion for chiropractic services. It may take you a bit of time to figure out why:

Benefits will not be paid for:
Services rendered by noncovered providers such as chiropractors, except in medically underserved areas.

Notice that the plan doesn't say it won't cover chiropractic services. It only says it won't pay for services rendered by chiropractors. But, since chiropractors are the guys who typically render chiropractic services, well, you figure out the rest.

All plans, both restrictive and lenient, hang their hats on the words "medically necessary." In fact, "medically necessary" is the Major Big Deal in health insurance and managed care. If a service, treatment, drug, or procedure ain't medically necessary, it ain't getting paid. If it is medically necessary, it may get paid—at least there's a fighting chance.

Superman Meets the Insurance Industry

On Memorial Day 1995, Christopher Reeve—an actor well known for his role as Superman—broke his neck in a horseback-riding accident in Culpeper, Virginia. He was left unable to move or breathe without assistance. Since then, Reeve has been forced to battle his insurance company for basic medical needs. He has become a champion of patient rights, and an inspiration to all.

The following is reprinted with permission from *Still Me*, by Christopher Reeve (Random House 1998).

My original discharge date from Kessler [a rehabilitation institute] was during the second week of November, but Dr. Kirshblum had convinced my insurance company to let me stay another month in response to my initiative about breathing.

Getting permission to stay longer in rehab was a major victory in our ongoing battles about insurance. During most of my stay at Kessler, Dr. Kirshblum, Dana, and I had to spend a tremendous amount of time writing passionate letters, fighting for reimbursement for medical necessities. The first major struggle was over nursing hours: the company wanted to pay for only forty-five days of home care, with a nurse on duty from 7:00 A.M. to 3:00 P.M. Outside those hours they expected Dana to be responsible for my care. They also refused to pay for a backup ventilator. Their argument was that if the vent failed, I could be kept alive by a nurse or Dana using an ambu bag while another ventilator was brought over from the supplier's office in Hawthorne, half an hour away. But the person on call for such emergencies might live in another town, as far as an hour away. And of course if the vent failed while I was out of town on a speaking engagement (my major source of income), I would be left in an impossible situation because you can't talk while you are being "bagged." The company even claimed that it was unnecessary for me to travel.

But what angered me most about the insurance company's position was their refusal to pay for any exercise equipment. Countless researchers have emphasized the importance of preparing the body for new treatments and therapies. If the muscles are allowed to atrophy, or if there is a significant loss of bone density because of inactivity, if the diaphragm is not exercised, then the patient will not be able to benefit from the progress scientists are making. In my case the company would not pay for any physical therapy work below the shoulders.

One of the reasons that insurance companies deny essential equipment and care is because only 30 percent of patients and their families fight back. While this allows the insurers to save enormous amounts of money, they would save even more by providing patients with the things they need: in most cases patients would improve dramatically or even be cured and no longer require costly reimbursements.

This exclusion can be found in various places throughout a plan. For example, as demonstrated in Step One, the composite plan in Appendix A includes this exclusion in the subsection labeled Authorizations, as well as in the Benefits section and the General Exclusions section and others.

Another extremely important exclusion, and one found in most health plans, is the exclusion for experimental and investigational drugs, devices, procedures, or treatments. This definition may have the power of life and death, including the power to control whether a person diagnosed with cancer can receive the benefits of cutting-edge, and controversial, scientific treatments.

In the composite plan set forth in Appendix A, this exclusion is found in the General Exclusions section that applies to *all* plan benefits. Then the term "experimental or investigational" is defined in the Definitions section as follows:

Experimental or investigational—A drug, device, or biological product is experimental or investigational if the drug, device, or biological product cannot be lawfully marketed without approval of the U.S. Food and Drug Administration (FDA) and approval for marketing has not been given at the time it is furnished. Approval means all forms of acceptance by the FDA.

A medical treatment or procedure, or a drug, device, or biological product is experimental or investigational if (1) reliable evidence shows that it is the subject of ongoing phase I, II, or III clinical trials or under study to determine its maximum tolerated dose, its toxicity, its safety, its efficacy, or its efficacy as compared with the standard means of treatment or diagnosis; or (2) reliable evidence shows that the consensus among experts regarding the drug, device, or biological product or medical treatment or procedure is that further studies or clinical trials are necessary to determine its maximum tolerated dose, its toxicity, its safety, its efficacy, or its efficacy as compared with the standard means of treatment or diagnosis [emphasis supplied].

Reliable evidence shall mean only published reports and articles in the authoritative medical and scientific literature; the written protocol or protocols used by the treating facility or the protocol(s) of another facility studying substantially the same drug, device, or medical treatment or procedure; or the written informed consent used by the treating facility or by another facility studying substantially the same drug, device, or medical treatment or procedure.

Determination of experimental/investigational status may require review of appropriate government publications such as those of the National Institutes of Health, National Cancer Institute, Agency for Health Care Policy and Research, Food and Drug Administration, and National Library of Medicine. Independent evaluation and opinion by Board Certified Physicians who are professors, associate professors, or assistant professors of medicine at recognized United States Medical Schools may be obtained for their expertise in subspecialty areas.

The key part of this definition is the part that's highlighted. Serious coverage disputes arise all the time from denials based on this exclusion. These disputes often end up in hotly contested lawsuits, especially when the benefits at issue are extremely expensive.

If you find yourself dealing with a serious health problem such as cancer, and facing a coverage denial on grounds that the requested treatment is experimental or investigational, this is probably one of the times where you should not hesitate to contact an attorney, preferably one experienced in battling insurance companies. One of the organizations listed in Appendix D may even be able to help you find one. If you're considering an experimental or investigational treatment, there's some chance that you're dealing with a deadly disease. There may be no time to waste.

2. THE DEFINITIONS

The Definitions section is a very quirky place to hide coverage exclusions. But read this section carefully; you're almost sure to find some there.

I think of definitions like the symbol pi. If you remember your high school algebra, you may remember that there was a little symbol, which I always thought looked a bit like an n, and which stood for the number 3.14.

Why did they call this number pi? No particular reason that I ever heard about. Maybe it was convenient, since they could use pi instead of writing out the actual number.

It's the same, sometimes, with definitions. Insurance companies occasionally pick words that they like, then define them to have meanings that serve their purposes. The trouble comes when the definitions and the words don't match, so the words don't mean what you think they do. The definition of "Accidental Injury" is a great example. It's certainly not intuitive to assume that the term "Accidental Injury" would exclude "injury to the teeth while eating." The insurance company that drafted the policy just decided that it would, since the insurance company chose not to cover it. But when you checked your policy to see if your cracked tooth was covered, you didn't bother to check the definition. You didn't think you needed to, because you thought you knew what Accidental Injury meant.

Another good example is the definition of "Reasonable and Customary." The definition shown in the composite policy in Appendix A states:

Reasonable and Customary: Those charges that are comparable to charges made by other providers for similar services and supplies under comparable circumstances in the same geographic area.

It all sounds perfectly reasonable and scientific, doesn't it? The problem is that it may not work out that way in practice. In fact, there's considerable risk that some of the final numbers may end up out of proportion to what doctors actually charge.

The best way to understand your definitions is to read them—a lot. Read them over and over, paying attention to every word. Words in contracts are there for a reason; except in rare cases, nothing got in by accident.

You also should pay attention to what is missing. If something is missing from the definitions, it may be missing from your coverage. Omission is like a shark below the surface of the water: you can't see it, but it's every bit as deadly.

3. THE LIMITATIONS

Another common trap for the unwary is the Limitations section. Every policy has one. When you first read this section, it may just look like a bunch of unimportant technicalities. It's not.

A common limitation, for example, is the statement that this policy may not pay claims if another policy is involved. This situation arises, for example, whenever people are hurt in car accidents. At times, it's unclear whether their medical costs are paid by auto insurance policies or health insurance policies. Many health plans treat these conflicts as exclusions. For example, one health plan excludes:

Any Covered Services that are payable as personal injury benefits under mandatory no-fault automobile insurance. Where permitted by state law, any Covered Services which are eligible for payment under the provisions of an automobile insurance contract or pursuant to any federal or state law which mandates indemnification for such services to persons suffering bodily injury from motor vehicle accidents.

Other plans call this a limitation, rather than an exclusion, and offer the following, lengthy explanation:

This coordination of benefits (double coverage) provision applies when a person covered by this Plan also has, or is entitled to benefits from, any other group health coverage, or is entitled to the payment of medical and hospitals costs under no-fault or other automobile insurance that pays benefits without regard to fault. Information about the other coverage must be disclosed to this Plan.

When there is double coverage for covered benefits, other than emergency services from non-Plan providers, this Plan will continue to provide its benefits in full, but is entitled to receive payment for the services and supplies provided, to the extent that they are covered by the other coverage, no-fault or other automobile insurance or any other primary plan.

One plan normally pays its benefits in full as the primary payer, and the other plan pays a reduced benefit as the secondary payer. When this Plan is the secondary payer, it will pay the lesser of (1) its benefits in full or (2) a reduced amount which, when added to the benefits payable by the other coverage, will not exceed reasonable charges. The determination of which health coverage is primary (pays its benefits first) is made according to guidelines provided by the National Association of Insurance Commissioners. When benefits are payable under automobile insurance, including no-fault, the automobile insurer is primary (pays its benefits first) if it is legally obligated to provide benefits for health care expenses without regard to other health benefits coverage the enrollee may have.

This provision applies whether or not a claim is filed under the other coverage. When applicable, authorization must be given this Plan to obtain information about benefits or services available from the other coverage, or to recover overpayments from other coverages.

From this lengthy explanation, here are the basic facts you need to know:

1. One of these two insurance plans should pay your medical costs.

2. The fight between the two of them should not be your problem.

3. Your health insurer has promised you that, when there is double coverage, it will pay full benefits for everything except certain emergency services.

4. You have promised to give your health insurer the authorization that it needs to seek reimbursement from the other insurer, if your insurer pays first but the other one was supposed to do so.

A similar conflict can arise when subscribers are eligible for Medicare. Medicare is a government-sponsored health plan, funded with money from Social Security taxes. Everyone over age sixty-five (and younger people with certain specified conditions) is eligible to participate, and many do so.

Many health plans have provisions pertinent to Medicare, including that they will only pay the amounts authorized by Medicare for persons who are eligible for the program. This provision often is expressed as a limitation, and it often can be hard to find. Other limitations involve claims that can be paid by Medicaid or by someone's third-party liability insurance policy or by other government agencies. It's a good idea to read, and pay attention to, all of these provisions.

CONCLUSION

All too often, Insurance companies give with one hand and, with the other, they take away. When they give, they call it benefits. When they take away, they have lots of different names.

It really doesn't matter what they call it, though, as long as you can: (1) find it; (2) understand it; and (3) figure out whether or not it applies. You're well on your way to doing all of these things, and to taking charge of your health care once and for all.

A LITTLE FINE-TUNING

KNOW THE TRUE COSTS OF YOUR HEALTH PLAN—THE PREMIUM ALONE IS *NOT* THE ANSWER

It's not easy to figure out the true costs of a health plan. There are many different kinds of costs: some obvious, some subtle—and some completely hidden.

Before you pick a health plan, you should try to find out about all of these costs. Otherwise you may have some very expensive surprises throughout the year. And most people don't have room in their budgets for such surprises, particularly ones that they could have avoided if they did their homework when they picked their health plans.

So—attention, class. Your homework assignment for this evening is to read this chapter and learn what a health plan is really going to cost you.

1. THE PREMIUM

The most obvious cost of any health plan is the premium. Most plans are pretty clear about that one. Since *your* premium dollar is *their* principal source of income, they want to make it perfectly clear that you will have to pay it.

Insurance companies struggle to make their premiums attractive. They know what we all know: that health insurance takes a sizable chunk out of many budgets and that people—especially healthy ones—are drawn to low premiums.

They also know something that most people don't know: a low premium can be balanced out by hidden, out-of-pocket costs.

Usually, health plans offer a number of choices when it comes to setting a premium. The alternatives typically vary depending upon the number of people in a family and the frequency of payments.

Another common variable involves the type of coverage selected. For example, an HMO plan with a POS option may offer two sets of premium choices: one reflecting the premium choices for the HMO-only plan and one reflecting the premium choices for the HMO plan with the POS option. And if there are other alternatives, such as a supplemental dental plan, there may be even more choices.

It's not too hard to figure out your premium, once you decide which options you want. It's even easy to compare the premiums of a number of different plans. Just pick out the premium number for approximately the same benefits for all of the plans that you may be considering, then compare them. No special skills required.

The problem is not in comparing premiums—it's keeping track of the less obvious, and even hidden, costs. Here are the main culprits.

2. THE FEE SCHEDULE

The most important financial information behind any health plan is how much the health plan is willing to pay for medical treatments and services. How much for an initial doctor's visit? How much for delivering a baby? How much for open-heart surgery? These questions are critical for both managed care plans and for typical indemnity plans.

Fees typically are paid based on a uniform coding system maintained by the American Medical Association. The codes used are called CPT codes, which stands for "current procedural terminology." There is a CPT code for every type of medical procedure, including an office visit, delivering a baby, and open-heart surgery. CPT codes usually consist of five digits, or a letter followed by four digits.

Whenever you see a doctor, your visit is broken down into CPT codes. Sometimes one code characterizes the entire visit; sometimes there is a group of codes. Your insurance company pays a preset fee for each of these codes, set forth on a fee schedule. A plan's fees can vary by region, by Zip Code and by other categories. If your insurance company decides to pay the bill for your visit, it is supposed to pay the preset fee for each code.

You may know more than you think about these CPT codes. Whenever you visit a doctor outside of a network, you may have gotten a sheet of paper filled with preprinted type. Your doctor should have checked off certain boxes, indicating the services he or she performed that day. The checked boxes contained CPT codes.

Fee schedules vary *widely*. The following chart, maintained by a doctor in New York City, sets forth the standard fees that were paid by particular plans at one time:

Sample Health Plans

Service	ABC	DEF	GHI	JKL	MNO	PQR
45-Minute Office Visit with New Patient (99204)	$97	$60	$110	N/A	$84	$125
60-Minute Office Visit with New Patient (99205)	$170	$70	$137	N/A	$94	N/A
10-Minute Office Visit with Existing Patient (99212)	$31	$35	$29	N/A	N/A	$22
15-Minute Office Visit with Existing Patient (99213)	$47	$40	$42	$54	$42	$47.80
25-Minute Office Visit with Existing Patient (99214)	$63	$45	$63	$64	N/A	N/A
40-Minute Office Visit with Existing Patient (99215)	$90	$50	$100	N/A	N/A	$115.20

This chart shows that some plans paid more than twice as much as others for exactly the same services. For example, the PQR plan paid $125 for a forty-five-minute office visit with a new patient, while the DEF plan paid only $60. Similarly, the ABC plan paid $170 for a sixty-minute office visit with a new patient, while the DEF plan paid only $70.

It also shows how coding works. A ten-minute visit with an existing patient has one code; a fifteen-minute visit has another code; and so on.

Whenever I work with CPT codes, I remember that Eskimos are supposed to have about eighty different words for snow. Maybe the Eskimos would understand why modern-day managed care plans need to have fifteen different codes for office visits.

Before you pick a health plan, you should find out as much as you can about its fee schedule. This information is invaluable, even if you are on a conventional HMO where you're not supposed to pay more than a premium and a minimal co-payment for each in-network visit. The value is that you can get a clue, in advance, of how well the plan pays its in-network doctors.

That information is important because, for one thing, it is likely to influence the quality of the doctors who apply to the network. Needless to say, the most prestigious doctors may choose to avoid the bargain-basement plans. And at least some doctors are really good at figuring out which plans pay the most.

Information about fee schedules will also be invaluable if you ever face paying your own bills and then seeking reimbursement, either on an out-of-network option or on a traditional indemnity plan. The fee schedule will reveal what the health plan thinks is the "usual and customary" fee in your area. That means it will dramatically affect the reimbursements that you will be able to receive.

If you have ever submitted a reimbursement form to an insurance company, you know all too well about the mysterious haircuts that show up on your Explanation of Benefits forms, commonly known as EOBs. Like—you pay a doctor $75 and think, naively, that you'll get back a percentage of $75. Instead, you receive reimbursement of a percentage of $45. All kinds of lingo are used to explain how $30 disappeared into the pockets of the insurance company, like "above usual and customary" and "maximum amount permitted." It all adds up to the same thing; you're out the money and they've got it.

If you bother to call for an explanation, you usually get more of the same. A typical answer is: "We don't pay any more than that because we have determined that to be the usual and customary rate in your area." But you knew that from the EOB before you made the phone call.

Most insurance companies are extremely reluctant to reveal the exact data they use to calculate what rates were "usual and customary." They also are reluctant to reveal the backup documentation that supports their final conclusions. No surprise, but it sometimes seems as if the person who set the rates hasn't a clue what the doctors are charging. This sometimes gives the impression that "usual and customary" is a self-fulfilling prophecy; it really means "the rates that *we intend to make* usual and customary, because they're the only rates that we intend to pay."

Sure, it's business as usual for a company to set the rates that it intends to pay its employees or its independent contractors. But that is not exactly what's happening here. This is different, for one thing, because third parties are heavily involved; it's the patients, after all, who pay the insurance premiums and who receive the services for which the rates are set.

It's also different because terms like "usual and customary" sound, at least to laymen, as though the rates accurately reflect the fees that actually are paid in circumstances outside of the network. These terms do *not* reveal the practical reality, which seems to be that these rates are little more than contract terms set by the insurer as a condition for being in the network.

The rates that insurance companies pay usually are set forth on internal documents known as fee schedules. Fee schedules set forth, by CPT code and geographic location, exactly how much the health plan will pay for each and every covered service, treatment, medication, and supply.

When you need to assess what a health plan really costs, you'll need to know the fee schedule. Otherwise, when you submit a $75 bill, you'll have no idea whether to expect reimbursement of $75, $62.50, $34.72, or any other random number. You won't know what you paid for; you won't know what you're entitled to receive; and you won't even know when you're being underpaid.

The problem is that many insurance companies seem to like it this way. Many of them refuse to let their consumers see their fee schedules; at least, they come up with all sorts of reasons why they can't.

Most common is confidentiality. "That information is confidential, for competitive purposes," a claims service representative may explain mysteriously.

This is nonsense. There's nothing inherently "confidential" about insurance company fee schedules. Retailers know what their competition is charging. Professionals can easily find out each other's billing rates. We all know how much the health plans ask us to pay in premiums. It is ridiculous for them to refuse to say how much they intend to pay of our claims.

Also, the information isn't even necessarily confidential. Many states require insurance companies to post certain fee schedules with insurance or health departments. With some digging, and a few Freedom of Information Act requests, you may be able to obtain some of this information.

Another excuse is that the information changes so frequently that it's impossible to commit it to a particular fee.

More nonsense. A fee schedule is not like the stock ticker, where prices vary from one instant to the next. Insurance companies are huge institutions; they ponderously set the particular fees that they intend to pay for services, treatments, medications, and supplies, and the amounts are known quantities.

Still another excuse is that there are so many fees, and so many regions, that it's too hard to answer any questions about the fee schedule.

That's just not true. Most people aren't interested in every single fee paid by health plans. They just need to know the health plan's fees for the services that they are most likely to need. A young couple planning a family may want to know the fees for childbirth and maternity care. A couple who already has children may want to know common pediatric fees. Someone with a bad back may want to know the standard chiropractor fees. All of these questions could be easily and accurately answered, if the health plans cared to.

Remember—if you don't know a health plan's fees, then it's meaningless to know what percentage it promised to reimburse to you. Insurance companies talk extensively about "80–20" plans and "70–30" plans, but the talk has no meaning unless you know the base amount.

Just do the math. Seventy percent of a $100 charge is $70 if the fee schedule permits reimbursement of the full $100. But if the fee schedule limits reimbursement to $50, then an 80 percent scale leaves you behind.

Picking a health plan without knowing its fee schedule is like buying a car without knowing what it costs. It's like being told by a car salesman, "Decide whether you want the six-cylinder engine or the four. After you sign the contract, we'll tell you the price."

All that said, there are a few tricks for finding out what a health plan will pay.

First, ask them. Ask them, hound them, nag them. Try to get them to reveal just a few fees: the ones that are the most important to you. It only takes a few to get a sense of a health plan's overall pay scale.

Second, ask your employer for help, if you're buying insurance through work. The employer is paying substantial premiums and has much more clout than any individual employee. If you plan it right, your employer may be able to figure out something creative, like requiring the release of such information as a condition for selecting a particular health plan.

Third, ask around. Find out if you have friends, neighbors, or colleagues who used the plan in previous years. Ask them what fees the plan paid at that time for services that interest you. If possible, ask to see some old EOBs. You can often figure out their standard fees by studying the fees that they've actually paid.

Fourth, ask doctors—or, better yet, the administrators in their offices. The doctors (or their administrators) know better than anyone how much particular plans pay for particular services. Their livelihoods depend upon it.

In fact, most doctors are more than happy to sound off about HMOs and health insurers. They, along with other "providers," like laboratories and pharmacies, have been dramatically affected by the shift to managed care. Most of them would welcome the chance to steer their patients away from poorly regarded plans and into the better ones. And they will greatly appreciate your interest and concern.

Fifth, contact your state's insurance and health departments and ask them for publicly filed fee information. Consider filing a Freedom of Information request, if necessary. At least you'll have the information for next year.

It can be very frustrating to get information about a health plan's fee schedule, but it's well worth the effort. And remember, you're not the only person looking for this information. So when you get a few answers, unless you're bound by some negotiated requirement of confidentiality, you may even consider posting them on the Internet. You may help someone else and, someday, they may find a way to help you.

3. DEDUCTIBLES

Deductibles seem very straightforward. They are the amount that you must spend out of pocket every year before you start getting reimbursement on an out-of-network option or a classic indemnity plan.

That's all there is to it, if you're a single person. But if you're married, and if you add a few children to the mix, deductibles start to get very complicated.

"This patient has a rare form of medical insurance."

The reason is a concept called "family deductibles." Typically there is an individual deductible for every person in a family. That person must meet that deductible every year before reimbursement commences. Then there is also a family deductible. The family deductible sets a maximum, communal deductible per family per year. If certain members of the family go to doctors frequently, they can max out the deductible for the entire family. This could mean that other members of the family are entitled to reimbursement for their very first doctor visits of the year.

It works like this. Assume that there are five people in a family: mother, father, and three children. They have a conventional fee-for-service contract, without any managed care aspects. Each person in the family has a $300 deductible and the combined family deductible is $900.

The three children go to the doctor a lot. Each one quickly meets his or her individual deductible. Then the father gets the flu. He goes to a doctor and gets full reimbursement, without needing to meet his own $300 deductible. That's because the family deductible of $900 was satisfied by the individual $300 deductibles of the three children.

One problem is that it usually doesn't work as simply as in this example. That's because people don't meet their deductibles one at a time. More often, one person will meet his individual deductible and start getting full reimbursement while others are still assigning sums to their deductibles. Then midway through the calculations on a particular claim, the family deductible is satisfied, and the reimbursements for everyone are supposed to start to flow.

Another problem is that—despite the vast mathematical capacities of modern computers—many insurance companies seem completely incapable of getting deductibles right.

I discovered this a few years ago, when my insurance company assigned a claim in November to a deductible. Our children at that time ranged from infancy to elementary school, and my home away from home was our pediatrician's office. I knew that we definitely, positively, absolutely had maxed out our family deductible by then.

When I checked our records, I was right—by hundreds of dollars. We actually had maxed our family deductible months before, yet the insurance company had continued to assign claims for each of us to our individual deductibles.

It didn't take long to show the insurance company the mistake. I just reviewed, dollar by dollar, the amounts assigned to the deductible, and stopped when I reached the family maximum. As for the rest, I requested prompt reimbursement.

The insurance company agreed that it owed the money. But, for one reason after another, it just couldn't figure out how to reimburse me. My favorite of the excuses was that something called the "accumulator" was broken and they couldn't reimburse me until it was fixed.

The "accumulator," it seems, was a computer assigned to "accumulate" *my* money. No wonder they weren't fixing it.

(I came up with what I thought was the perfect solution. I told the customer service representative that I'd get my own accumulator. It would break down and start accumulating the insurer's money—and I wouldn't fix it either!)

It took more than a year of phone calls before I got complete reimbursement. By then, I was well into the next year's expenses. And, no surprise, I quickly discovered that the insurance company was doing it again.

So, when you're picking a health plan, pay attention to the money you'll spend on the individual and family deductibles. And, after you've purchased the plan, make sure that your deductible is not overcharged.

4. CO-PAYMENTS

Most times that you see a doctor, you are required to pay a fixed sum out of your own pocket. This sum is usually called a co-payment or coinsurance. In HMOs and PPOs, the sum is often $5 or $10, no matter what type of visit or service. In indemnity plans and when you go out of network on an HMO, the sum often is set by percentage. A typical co-payment is 20 percent of the doctor's charge, but co-payments are sometimes even higher.

Co-payments can add up to a lot of money, especially if you visit doctors often. Moreover, if you are outside of a network, they are in addition to deductibles, and also in addition to any difference that may exist between your doctor's actual charge and the fee that the plan is willing to pay.

The following health plan—an HMO with a POS option—offers a typical array of co-payments:

- For straight HMO care, either conducted by a primary care physician or referred by a primary care physician to an approved specialist, the co-pay for a standard office visit is $5.

- For mental conditions and substance abuse, the co-pay starts at $15 and increases to $25, then $35, depending on the number of office visits.

- There is no co-payment for in-patient hospitalization, but there is a co-payment of $25 for every emergency room visit.

- The co-payment for prescribed medication, filled at an in-network pharmacy, is $5 per prescription unit or refill.

- For out-of-network medical and surgical benefits, the co-payment is 20 percent.

- For out-of-network care for mental conditions and substance abuse, the co-payment is graduated. It starts at 20 percent, for the first five visits; increases to 35 percent through thirty visits; and becomes 50 percent for all other visits.

- Prescriptions written by an out-of network doctor and filled at an in-network pharmacy are subject to $5 co-payment.

- Prescriptions written by an out-of network doctor and filled at an out-of-network pharmacy are subject to a 20 percent co-payment.

- Failure to obtain precertification where it was required could result in the doubling of the 20 percent co-payment obligation.

It should be fairly obvious that co-payments can add up. That's what makes them a financial factor in every health plan. So make sure you find out about a plan's co-payments before you pick the plan—not after.

5. OUT-OF-POCKET MAXIMUMS

Most health plans set out-of-pocket maximums. For indemnity plans or out-of-network options, these maximums are fixed sums. Typically, once your deductibles and co-payments equal the out-of-pocket maximum, you no longer are required to make any co-payments. Instead, you become entitled to 100 percent reimbursement of all covered services.

Out-of-pocket maximums are not small numbers. A common out-of-pocket maximum in recent years was $1,000 per individual and $2,000 per family. A family with average health needs, in an unremarkable year, may not spend this much in out-of-pocket expenses.

Sometimes, though, it is very easy to meet this out-of-pocket maximum. For example, the maximum could easily be met in a year when a woman has a baby, and uses a doctor out of network. The maximum also could be met in a year with a major out-of-network surgery, or serious illness.

Under many plans, it is your responsibility to keep track of your out-of-pocket expenditures and to tell the health plan when the maximum has been met. The health plan will not switch to 100 percent reimbursement on its own initiative. This situation is roughly comparable to calculating the family deductible.

The term "out-of-pocket maximum" occasionally is used in connection with managed care plans, but it is a misnomer. No "maximum" is set for co-payments in these plans. The term is typically a way of reassuring you that you will not have to pay for anything except the premium and some minor co-payments.

6. LIFETIME MAXIMUMS

Many plans—especially plans purchased by individuals, as opposed to group plans purchased by employers—set lifetime maximums in addition to annual out-of-pocket maximums. These maximums can be catastrophic for your finances, especially if you suffer a catastrophic illness. A typical lifetime maximum is $1 million, which means that your health plan will not pay more than $1 million for your health care for your entire life.

For example, the following plan was filled with lifetime maximums—none of which would go very far:

- The Hospice benefit is limited to $7,500 per person per lifetime when the hospice care is precertified.

- The Hospice benefit is limited to $4,500 per person per lifetime when the hospice care is not precertified

- The Orthodontic benefit is limited to $1,000 per person per lifetime.

- The Substance Abuse benefit is limited to two treatment programs per person per lifetime.

- The Smoking Cessation benefit is limited to one per person per lifetime.

- Diagnosis and treatment of infertility is limited to a maximum benefit of $5,000 per person per lifetime.

While this particular plan did not specify a cap on mental health benefits, you should appreciate that such caps appear very frequently.

Lifetime maximums are a fact of life in many types of health plans. Make sure you know whether they are in your plan, and plan accordingly.

7. PAYMENT PENALTIES

It's always a good idea to skim a plan and search for hidden payment penalties. One example is the plan that reserves its rights to double your 20 percent co-payment obligation if you fail to obtain precertification for a service that required precertification. Such penalties can take any size, shape, or form, so you should be alert to this issue whenever you look over a plan.

8. OUT-OF-NETWORK REFERRALS

This is perhaps the most hidden issue of all.

If you see a doctor out of network and he orders you to have tests or see other specialists, the tests and additional doctors' bills usually will not be covered by your plan. This is so even if the tests are done at a location that belongs to the network and if the doctors to which you are referred participate in the network. If you want to get coverage, you usually must obtain a referral from a doctor on the plan—even if it means seeing a whole lot of extra doctors.

Don't forget this, or you could find yourself with a bunch of expensive lab charges or uncovered medical bills. It's fine to see a doctor out of network. But stop there, unless you're willing to accept that you might have to pay the freight yourself.

9. CAFETERIA PLANS

When it comes to the cost of health care, there's one more thing to keep in mind. Many companies offer their employees the opportunity to participate in "cafeteria plans," variously known as medical savings accounts and flexi-spending accounts. These can be terrific money savers, if you're smart about it.

In a cafeteria plan, you direct your company before January 1 of each calendar year to withdraw a certain amount of money, pretax, from your salary. Then you use these pretax dollars to pay for health care that is not covered by insurance. This means deductibles, coinsurance, co-payments, eyeglasses, contact lenses, dental care, orthodontia, and so on. You even can use pretax dollars to pay your health insurance premium.

It usually works on a reimbursement system. You incur a noncovered health expense and pay for it in cash, check, or credit card—meaning, out of posttax income. Then you submit your receipts to your employer, who reimburses you for the full amount from your own pretax dollars. You get to spend the pretax reimbursement money on anything you want. At the end of the day, you've saved the taxes that you would have paid on this money.

Here is an extreme oversimplification of how it works. If you are in a 30 percent tax bracket, let's assume you pay $30 in taxes for every $100 that you make. (It doesn't really work this way, but that doesn't matter.) You decide to put away $100 in your cafeteria plan. This means that you are putting away the *entire* $100, including the $30 that you otherwise would have paid in taxes.

You have a deductible of $100, meaning your health plan will not pay for your first $100 of covered expenses. You pay $100 of *posttax* income to your doctors, in order to exhaust this deductible. You submit proof of payment to your cafeteria plan and receive back a check for $100. The check comes out of $100 that you put away in pretax dollars.

Now you've basically paid your $100 deductible in pretax dollars, which includes the $30 that you avoided paying in taxes. So, after all of this, you've saved $30.

If you don't have a lot of uncovered medical expenses, then you won't save too much through a cafeteria plan. But whatever you save, it's worth it. There's no reason to pay money in taxes when you don't have to. And every little bit of savings helps.

There's only one trick—but it's a big one. The trick is that, if you overestimate, you will forfeit any unused money. At the end of the year, your employer will not take taxes out of the money left in your account, and pay it to you as regular income. Instead, it's use it or lose it.

Ordinarily it's not too hard to estimate your annual uncovered health care costs. Just add up the amount that was uncovered the previous year and use that as a guideline to anticipate the next year's expenses. Include the anticipated expense of events that you know will take place in the next year, such as root canals, orthodontia, cataract surgery, and the like. You can check the prices in advance with the doctors and dentists that you plan to use, so you're not just guessing.

When in doubt, estimate low. The tax savings that you achieve from cafeteria plans can be canceled out, and then some, if you forfeit more than a few dollars.

But don't worry too much. There's an easy solution if the "worst" happens—you have a healthier year than you anticipated and your balance at the end of the year is too high.

Go shopping. Buy a new pair of contact lenses; you'll need them soon enough. Prescription sunglasses? Why not? Do the dental work that you've been putting off; sorry, but you can't afford not to. If you think about your health care needs, you'll probably find lots of ways to spend that money.

The secret to a cafeteria plan is spending what you put aside. As long as you do that, cafeteria plans are great opportunities. If you're lucky enough to have one available to you, make sure that you use it.

CONCLUSION

If cost is important to you when shopping for health coverage, it would be a good idea to prepare a chart comparing the different costs of the health plans. The chart of a savvy shopper could look something like this:

Plan	Monthly Premium	Out-of-Network Deductibles	In-Network Co-payments	Out-of-Pocket Maximums	Lifetime Maximums
ABC FFS with PPO[1]	$64/person $188/family	$250/person $500/family $175/hospital visit	No such option	$2,500/ person $4,000/ family $4,000/ mental	$7,500/Hospice (precertified) $4,500/Hospice (not certified) $1,000 Orthodontic $5,000 Infertility Two programs: Substance Abuse One program: Smoking Cessation
DEF HMO with POS[2]	$52/person $186/family	$200/person $400/family [POS only]	$5/medical $15+/mental $5/hospital	$2,000/ person $4,000/ family [POS only]	None stated
GHI PPO with POS[3]	$28/person $62/family	$200/person $250/ nonnetwork hosp. visit $150/ nonnetwork outpat. care	$12/medical $25/mental [POS only]	$2,000/PPO $3,750/POS	None stated

[1]Meaning a traditional plan, where you pay the doctor and then submit a bill for reimbursement, with the option of using a select network of doctors to get a better deal.
[2]Meaning a traditional HMO, with an option of going out of network for a higher price.
[3]Meaning a plan requiring you to use a network of selected physicians, but allowing you to go outside for a higher price.

Sure, it looks like a lot of work. But it's easier than you think, especially because most plans have summary pages where you can find all of this financial information in one place. And it's a whole lot cheaper to do it this way than it is to get stuck with the wrong insurance policy.

"Open Season" Is Like Baseball Season: Three Strikes, and You're Out

My husband and I had a bright idea a few years back. We decided to change our health plan during the office's "open season."

We had decided to try an HMO in an attempt to cut down on our endless paperwork. But we also wanted the option of choosing our own doctors, so we wanted a plan with a POS option. We picked one and I dove into the POS section.

At first blush, it sounded great. It boasted, with distracting emphasis, "For eligible self-referral services, the *Plan pays* 80 percent of the allowable benefit after *you pay* a $200 calender year deductible for an individual, or $400 for a family." These deductibles were low, and the percentages high.

But then I reread the subtle words: "allowable benefit."

The plan, you see, was not promising to pay 80 percent of what is billed by out-of-network doctors. It only sounded that way. All the plan was doing was promising to pay, basically, 80 percent of what it feels like paying.

I realized that, to understand what this plan really offered, I needed to know what the "allowable benefits" would be. So I picked a straightforward example—a run-of-the-mill pediatrician visit—and tried to find out what would be "allowed."

Surprise, surprise—I never got this information. And, when I later told some doctors about my efforts, they laughed at me for even trying.

On my first call, it took me a long time to explain to a customer service representative what I wanted to find out. Once I passed that hurdle, he said he had absolutely no idea. Then he disconnected me, while supposedly trying to transfer me to someone else.

Strike one.

On my second call, a different rep told me she couldn't answer the question in a vacuum. She'd need to see an exact bill, filled in with specific billing codes, to tell me the price.

(continued)

I explained that this was impossible, since I hadn't joined the plan yet. She urged me to do so, since that would be the only way for me to get this information.

Strike two.

Being a persistent type, I gave it one more try. I called back again and reached yet another representative. This time I offered to send in a blank, standard-form bill listing a wide variety of standardized codes. I asked the representative if she would fill in the prices. This representative promised to ask her supervisor and call me back.

She called the next day, and left a cheery message on my voice mail, explaining that "actual charges vary from moment to moment," so they couldn't answer my question in advance. The bottom line was that to get an answer, I'd have to join the plan and start submitting actual claims.

Strike three, and I was out—of luck, time, and patience.

At the end of the day, the only way I could find out what the plan would pay as an "allowable benefit" would be to sign up for an entire year, then wait for the denials.

I recently was on a talk show with an insurance lobbyist who complained that people spend less time picking their health plans than they do buying their cars.

Well, maybe that's true. But if it is, insurance companies must like it that way. If they didn't, they would be more forthcoming with hardworking consumers who are simply trying to learn the score.

THE DEVIL IS IN THE DETAILS—
BE SMART ABOUT OPTIONS, CUSTOMER
SERVICE, AND MORE

When it comes to picking a health plan, don't lose track of the basics: issues like which type of plan suits your needs, what it covers, how much it pays for services rendered, how expensive it is, and so on. But once you've found a plan that suits these needs, the next step is to consider secondary issues.

These secondary issues include options that may be offered by the plan, such as dental coverage, vision coverage, disability coverage, and long-term care. They include what doctors, hospitals, and laboratories are used by the plan, and how the plan is ranked by various organizations and consumer groups. They also include mundane, but incredibly important, details like the quality of the plan's customer service department, how long you'll wait for reimbursement, and how long you'll wait on hold.

1. COVERAGE OPTIONS

Many health plans, and many employers, offer options to purchase additional types of coverage, such as dental, vision, and disability coverage. Here are some issues to consider:

A. Dental Coverage

Most health plans offer limited dental coverage, such as coverage for certain types of injuries to teeth. That doesn't rank as true dental coverage. A real dental plan covers things like annual checkups, filling cavities, root canal—all that stuff that makes you hide from your dentist.

These plans often sound much better than they are. Generally they offer very limited benefits at a relatively high cost. They also seem to pay extremely low fees for dental services, which means that very few dentists seem to participate in these plans.

Also, if you know in advance that you need a root canal, or another dental procedure, read the plan very carefully before you buy it. Insurance companies are well aware that people often go shopping for dental coverage after they find out they need an expensive procedure. So dental plans typically contain all kinds of restrictions, like particularly long waiting periods before they'll pay for these procedures. That's okay if you're planning ahead, but it can be a real problem if you need the procedure soon.

By now you're probably well equipped to determine what is really covered under a dental plan. As discussed in Steps One to Three, start out by reading the Benefits section, then start hunting for exclusions and limitations. Along the way, pay attention to the dental plan's definitions. See, you've become an expert.

B. Vision Coverage

It's almost exactly the same deal with vision coverage. The concept is great; the delivery is often disappointing. Beware of buying an expensive vision plan that never really covers what you need.

C. Disability Coverage

In most cases, people who become disabled never thought it would happen to them. That means that if they bought disability insurance, they probably did not spend much time reading their policies until after they became disabled.

Short-term disability is provided by many employers. It typically provides up to 60 percent of an ordinary salary for between three to six months. Pregnancy and maternity leaves may be treated as short-term disabilities under these policies. Thus, you should be entitled to short-term disability payments even if you are not given a paid maternity leave—assuming your employer offers such coverage in the first place.

Long-term disability insurance is another matter. Some employers provide this coverage in addition to short-term coverage, but more and more consumers have been buying these policies privately. These policies vary widely and should be studied very carefully before you select one. The differences include the percentage of the predisability income that is paid by the disability insurer whether the benefits are tax free or taxable; and whether the benefits will be paid for a claimant's lifetime in terms of working years, or for a limited period of time.

For some reason, many disability policies are even harder to read than ordinary health plans. Also, it can be even harder to recover on a disability claim than a health claim in many cases.

One common denial asserted by disability insurers is that the claimant is physically capable of working, but is choosing not to as a lifestyle matter. Another is that the claimant simply is refusing to take reasonable actions to minimize his or her physical limitations, and thereby enable him or her to go back to work. A third is that the pain, discomfort, and other issues that supposedly prevent the claimant from working do not find support in the medical records.

If you've ever filed a disability claim, you may be all too familiar with some, if not all, of these arguments. If you're new to the game, here are some of the rules.

First, work closely with your doctors. You may never win a disability claim unless your doctors create a good record, showing that you truly are suffering from a medical condition (it can be physical or mental) that prevents you from working. Your doctors probably will need to write several letters: an initial letter explaining your condition; a second letter in response to particular questions from the disability insurer; and a third letter that addresses the conclusions reached by the insurer's doctors.

Your doctor's letters are of critical importance since your doctors know more about your condition than anyone else does. They certainly know more than the insurance company doctors who do nothing except review your medical charts and test results, without seeing you. Most courts know this; in fact, courts often hold that the recommendations of your doctors (called treating physicians) carry more weight than the recommendations of doctors who have never seen you (called nontreating physicians).

Second, be aware that many disability insurers are into surveillance. Yes, this means spies. It is not unheard-of for disability insurers to hire spies to figure out whether a person who claims to be disabled really is disabled. These spies may follow you on a weekend afternoon, making notes about what you do and where you go. They may even hide in the bushes and take pictures. (Creepy, isn't it?) Their goal, of course, will be to prove that you are not as disabled as you say.

Third, think creatively about how to prove your limitations. Disability insurers may ask you to send them any information you want them to see regarding your physical limitations. Don't bother asking them to be more specific; it's not their job to help you prove your case.

At this point, you should try to think beyond doctors' reports about your health problems and income statements showing that you're making less money. Think about whether you wrote any memos to your employer explaining your physical limitations. Think about whether you ever wrote to business associates or customers, explaining that you can no longer perform your customary duties. Think about other actions that may reveal changes in your physical abilities, such as sports teams from which you may have resigned, health clubs where you may have dropped your membership, vacations that you may have canceled, and so on. Tell your disability insurer about all of this; it may greatly improve your chances of winning your claim.

D. Long-Term Care

If you ever think of buying coverage for long-term care— watch out. Long-term care is evolving and changing rapidly, and you should be sure that any policy you purchase is up to date.

Some plans, for example, limit long-term care to nursing homes, usually through the Definitions section. They state that you will have coverage, subject to certain amounts and terms, if you are in a nursing home.

But as most people are well aware, there are lots of long-term care alternatives that don't involve nursing homes. They include home health aides, assisted-living facilities, and other creative options. None of these are necessarily included under plans that cover nursing homes.

Most modern plans, however, offer an option to cover these developing alternatives. Make sure that you understand what these options are all about before you make any decisions.

Here's the bigger issue. Because long-term insurance is a brand-new animal, insurance companies usually are not willing to guarantee your premium rates for the rest of your life. Presumably this is because no one knows what the costs of long-term care will be in the future, as the population ages.

Many people may think (to the extent that they think about it at all) that buying long-term insurance when they're young will enable them to lock in a low rate forever. That's basically how it works in life insurance. For long-term care insurance, it may be true as well—but not necessarily. Unlike life insurers, long-term care insurers do not promise that they will never change your premium in the future.

So if you decide to buy long-term care insurance at all, make sure you know what you're getting.

2. DETAILS THAT RUN YOUR LIFE

Health plans differ in important ways. Some pay claims on time. Others are notorious slow payers. Some have reasonably efficient customer service systems. For others, you could pass away while on hold—and no one would notice.

These details will affect the quality of your life, or at least the part of your life spent fighting with your health insurer. So pay attention to them when you're picking a health plan.

One way to judge a health plan is to call customer service and set a timer. Record how long you are on the phone before you speak to an actual person. Ask a specific question, such as how much the health plan will pay for a particular service in your Zip Code (see Step Four). Then see whether you ever get the answer, or at least see what it takes for the health plan to refuse to answer the question.

To be fair, try not to judge a plan on a single experience with customer service. Try it at least twice, on different days and at different times. After that, you'll have a fairly clear idea of what it will be like to deal with this particular health plan.

It's also smart, when picking a health plan, to pay special attention to its rules regarding emergencies. This topic has already been discussed in Step Two, when we analyzed the various Benefits sections. What's important to remember is that you should look for a plan with flexible rules regarding notification, and that trusts your judgment when it comes to deciding what's really an emergency.

Even if you are conscious and alert, you still may forget to call your health plan in the first few hours after an emergency. Look for a plan that accommodates this reality, not one that takes advantage of it.

Another issue to consider is whether a plan will permit you to change primary care physicians in the middle of the policy year. This issue can become very important if you are unhappy with the doctor that you chose. You obviously would not want to be stuck for an entire year with such a doctor. Not every plan, however, would allow you to switch. Find out whether the plan you choose is one of them.

Another important consideration is the quality of the doctors who participate in a health plan. At the end of the day, if the doctors are great, it seems that many people will endure incredibly inefficient bureaucracies.

Before you join a health plan, you should find out what doctors participate in that plan. If you know any of them, you should immediately call them to confirm that they still are on the plan, and to ask them how they like it.

This is extremely important because the roster of physicians on a health plan can change at any time. Just because a health plan says that certain doctors are on its plan doesn't

mean that it's right. If it's wrong, the time to find out is *before* you sign up, not after.

Doctors get into disputes with plans, and either drop out or are terminated all the time. If trouble is brewing, it's best if you find out about it before you commit to the plan. Many doctors are forthright about these situations when asked direct questions. And even if they don't want to talk about it, you lose nothing by asking.

Further, it's usually bad to join a health plan that has a chronic problem with its doctors. You can end up stuck with a plan, and having one primary care physician after another drop out. A conversation with your doctor about his or her feelings about a plan may steer you away from a plan that the medical community thinks is rotten. Such a conversation could save you considerable irritation in the future, and would be well worth your time.

Yet another way to judge a health plan is by the timing of

its payments, either to your doctor or to you. There are a few ways of getting this information. The first one is word of mouth. Ask people who are, or were once, on the plan what they experienced in this regard. Make sure to ask doctors, too; their records and recollections may be quite reliable.

Second, contact local organizations, including the state insurance and health departments, consumer organizations, and local medical societies. Any or all of these organizations may keep tabs on the payment history of health plans, and they should be more than happy to share their findings with you.

Third, check your local newspaper as well as the Internet. Chronically slow payments by insurance companies may have hit the news. A medical society in New York, for example, commenced a class action lawsuit against one health plan for a notoriously slow payment history, and the lawsuit quickly achieved favorable results. If a plan has a very bad (or a very good) track record, it should be relatively easy to find out.

You can and should follow these same steps to find out about the plan's practices with regard to denials in general. It won't take much research for you to discover whether a plan is trigger-happy when it comes to issuing denials. If it has a bad reputation in this area, you may find that it denies your claims too.

Finally, if you hear too many horror stories, perhaps you should not buy the plan. This may seem obvious, but unfortunately it's not. Often people are beguiled by a low premium or great-sounding coverage, so they develop selective hearing when it comes to the plan's flaws. Remember that the low premium won't make you happy if you end up with a file filled with coverage denials, grievances, and appeals. The same holds true for the coverage that sounded great on paper.

3. CONDITIONS THAT CAN DESTROY YOUR COVERAGE

Conditions involve mistakes that *you* can make, that can keep you from getting the coverage offered by the plan. The most-hated condition, which is found in most plans, probably is the requirement that you must call the plan for authorization before you head to an emergency room, or at least within a certain number of hours of your visit.

As discussed in Step One, these conditions can be traps for the unwary. So don't be the one who forgets to call your health plan in an emergency; you'll regret it for a long time.

In addition, conditions can be hard to find. Many health plans do not contain a single section called Conditions, or any variation of the term. But read the plan carefully—now that you're an expert, you'll find them.

Here's a great example of a hard-to-find condition. It's in the section called Facts About This Plan:

> **HOSPITAL CARE** **If you require hospitalization, your primary care doctor or authorized specialist will make the necessary arrangements and continue to supervise your care.**

Get it? It's hard to see. The condition is that you can't go to an emergency room unless you first get permission from one of your doctors on the plan.

The condition is explained further in the Emergency Benefits section. There the plan gives you the option of going straight to a hospital in "extreme emergencies, if you are unable to contact your doctor. . . ." Be very careful, though. You and the plan may have different opinions about what is "extreme." You may also disagree about how hard you were supposed to try—in the middle of the crisis—to contact your primary care doctor.

A related condition—the source of many disputes—is the requirement of precertification for certain expensive services and procedures, including hospital care. This is the stuff that scandals are made of. Some health plans have become infamous for refusing to precertify medical treatments in certain desperate situations. While everyone fights about precertification, the patient sickens and dies.

One recent case involved a woman named Judith Packiewicz, in New York. She suffered from liver cancer and was believed to need a transplant to have any chance at survival. Her insurance company denied coverage until the eleventh hour. When it changed its mind, she was rushed into surgery—only to die on the operating table.

Precertification requirements have endless pitfalls. The following plan gives some examples:

PRECERTIFY BEFORE ADMISSION	**Precertification is not a guarantee of benefit payments. Precertification of an inpatient admission is a predetermination that, based on the information given, the admission meets the medical necessity requirements of the Plan. It is your responsibility to ensure the precertification is obtained.**
NEED ADDITIONAL DAYS?	**If any additional days are required, your physician or the hospital must request certification for the additional days. If the admission is precertified but you remain confined beyond the number of days certified as medically necessary, the Plan will not pay for charges incurred on any extra days that are determined not to be medically necessary by the Carrier during the claim review.**

Now, let's see. First, even if they precertify you, they may not be obligated to pay your claims. Second, the precertification formalities may be entirely your responsibility. Third, if you make any mistakes, you may get financially penalized. Fourth, if you need extra days, it may be your job to get them precertified—even though you're in the hospital and presumably too ill to go home. You get the idea.

There are, however, ways to protect yourself against these conditions.

When you join a health plan, familiarize yourself completely with all of these prerequisites to coverage. Read them over and make sure you understand them. Don't just read the words without really paying attention.

I'm not suggesting that you should memorize all of these prerequisites. But if you read them and understand them at the beginning, there's a good chance that you'll remember they exist at the critical moment. All you really need is the thought that maybe you'd better check your plan before taking any action. That thought may be enough to keep you from making a mistake that may be fatal to your coverage.

Another trick is to type up an index card that states what you must do before going to an emergency room. Put on the card all of the names, titles, and telephone numbers of the persons you must call, as well as the nature of the prerequisite. Also put down the names, addresses, and telephone numbers of the nearest participating hospitals, and driving directions if possible. Finally, put down the exact names and subscriber ID numbers of all members of your family.

Make at least four copies of this card. Keep one; give one to your spouse; give one to your baby-sitter or your mother or your adult child (any third party who's likely to be around in a crisis); and post the last one near the kitchen phone. That way, you won't fumble in a crisis. No matter where you are, you should be able to gain quick access to procedures that your health plan has set.

4. PLAY BY THEIR RULES

I've learned from personal experience, and from the experiences of my clients, that the best way to deal with insurance companies is to play by their rules. It's always great when you can say, "I've checked your procedures manual and I see that I have all of the symptoms that you think justify this particular procedure." It's kind of like saying "Checkmate."

Unfortunately the converse is also true. If you don't play by an insurance company's rules, you may find it impossible to get anything done. Everywhere you turn, you will bump into technicalities and burdensome, time-consuming requirements.

For this reason, you may be better off if you plan to use your health plan in the way it was designed to be used. Don't pretend your fee-for-service plan will give you the convenience of an HMO. Don't pretend your HMO will give you the flexibility of a fee-for-service plan.

Also, if you don't plan to use in-network doctors most of the time, then think carefully about whether you should pick an HMO—even when it offers a POS option.

HMOs are HMOs. The people who work there live, eat, and breathe network. The bureaucracy is geared toward network use. The idea of an out-of-network option is great—but it's often a rusty wheel that doesn't turn.

All kinds of terrible things seem to happen to people on HMOs who decide to go out of network. Like no one ever responds to their out-of-network claims. Or, when they respond, they treat patients as if they're doctors, and send the types of rejections that patients are never supposed to see. Or, if they do pay, they send the checks to the doctors instead of the patients. And so on.

It's much better to play by the rules, and make the rules work for you.

---

5. BECOME A PACKRAT

Insurance companies can be their own worst enemies. In their zeal to attract patients and doctors, they often boast in advertisements, brochures, and other written materials about the superior quality of their services, their bureaucracy, and their networks.

These advertisements may someday be very helpful to you. Many states, for example, place special, legal obligations upon insurance companies that engage, or are accused of engaging, in false or misleading advertising. If you can show that an insurance company's promotional materials were inaccurate, and that you suffered damages because you relied upon them, your insurance company may start writing a substantial check to you.

So when you first join a health plan, you should collect every single piece of paper that the plan sends to you: every brochure, every advertisement, every summary of coverage, everything. You also should collect every advertisement that you find about the plan on your own. Magazine and newspaper ads are good examples, as are pages printed from Web sites, and even letters sent to you on letterhead.

File it away in a safe place, preferably in the insurance file that is discussed in Step Six. You never know what may help you someday to prove your right to insurance coverage.

CONCLUSION

Little things can make a big difference when you join a health plan. Like how long your plan will take to answer the phone, send you a check, process a referral—or respond to your request for a liver transplant. It's a good idea to pay careful attention to these "little" things. One of them may save your life someday.

Not So Usual, Not So Customary

The first time that I really understood the endless reaches of the "usual and customary" game was when I was pregnant with our third child. My OB/GYN sent me for genetic testing. Since genetic testing is expensive, I knew that my insurance company probably would claim that the bill was "above the usual and customary" rates. I had found, by then, that insurance companies always seem to do this on the big bills.

I decided it was time to plan ahead. So I called every place that did genetic testing within a hour's drive from my home, and got a list of prices. I chose the cheapest one (which also was extremely reputable). I went there and had the test, and my insurance company got the bill.

It was immediately rejected as "above the usual and customary." And I was loaded for bear.

I called the insurance company and asked what they thought was the usual and customary charge. That, they said, was confidential. I asked them how they decided what was usual and customary. They said that was confidential too.

Then I told them about my price list, which forced them to reveal some more information. They explained that the issue was the charge for genetic counseling. That's when a trained counselor discusses with you the risks of genetic abnormalities and whether you would ever consider terminating a pregnancy.

That counseling, my insurance company explained, was nothing more than a typical office visit—say, for a sprained ankle. After all, it took place in an office.

That, quite frankly, struck me as ridiculous. A typical office visit? Just like a sprained ankle? Without getting into a debate about abortion rights, the analogy to a sprained ankle seemed way out of line.

A few days later, I received a bill from the unpaid hospital, telling me that they were turning over my account to collections. I responded

(continued)

by speaking with our genetics counselor, and telling her the story. Her role, I suggested, was not to fight with me over the shortfall in the payment. Instead, she needed to convince the insurance industry that the potential abortion of a genetically impaired fetus was different than a sprained ankle.

Because I had kept detailed records, I gave her the names, telephone numbers, and titles of everyone I had spoken to at the insurance company, and the dates and times of the conversations. I pointed her, in particular, to the woman who told me that genetic counseling is the same as a sprained ankle.

To my relief and, to some extent my surprise, I never heard any more about it—not from the genetics counselor, not from the hospital, and not from the insurance company. I never received another bill and no one ever turned me in to collections.

I'd like to think that something good happened behind the scenes. Maybe someone at the insurance company decided to change the codes for genetic counseling. Maybe institutionally the insurance company recognized that there really is a difference between genetic counseling and a sprained ankle.

Maybe. Or maybe they just decided that it was too much trouble. At this point, I'll probably never know.

Now—Make Them Pay!

"Sorry, folks, but your insurance doesn't pay cover
more than one day in the manger."

IF YOU WANT TO FIGHT A COMPUTER, YOU MUST BECOME A COMPUTER: ALWAYS KEEP VERY CAREFUL RECORDS

Does anyone remember *A Wrinkle in Time*? In case you don't, this is an extraordinary science fiction book that has fascinated children and adults for generations. If you haven't read it, you should; if you loved it as a child, it's worth reading again.

The evil protagonist in the book is a monstrous, pulsating, disembodied brain known as IT. (My apologies to all information technology specialists. The book was written in 1962, long before anyone even imagined your profession.) IT creates a "perfect" world, where everyone obeys the "Manual," examiners keep order, and the only thing lacking is humanity. IT comes close to destroying the warmhearted little family that the book is about.

It reminds me, at times, of health insurers.

Here's a secret—in certain respects, health insurers and HMOs are nothing more than computers. At least at the lower levels, most of the people who work there are interchangeable. The computers control.

You will have learned this already if you've ever had the following experience. You call the customer service department of an insurance company, push no less than fifteen numbers on your telephone key pad in response to computerized questions, listen to music for maybe ten minutes, finally have a live customer service representative pick up your call, and then spend some time explaining a complicated problem. The representative finally understands the problem, and agrees to take certain actions to solve it.

You wait a month, and nothing happens, so you call for a progress report. You eventually reach a different customer sales representative, who looks up your identification number in the computer. That person then informs you that no actions were taken; moreover, there is no record of any previous conversation.

After having this experience a few times too many, I learned how to talk to customer service departments and other departments at insurance companies. I talk only to their computers. At the beginning of every conversation, I ask the customer service representatives to enter into the computer that we are having a conversation, and to include the date and time. Then I listen for typing. After all, unless they're typing, they're not entering anything into the computer. If I don't hear typing, I point that out to them. The typing usually starts.

Throughout the conversation, I periodically ask the customer service representatives exactly what they are entering into the computer. I realize that what is getting entered may be much different from what I'm told. But, to a certain extent, it doesn't matter, as long as they are making some record of our conversation.

At the end of the conversation, I ask the representatives to explain what actions they plan to take, and when. Then I ask them to enter this information into the computer.

Customer service representatives don't particularly like this approach. I apologize profusely, and explain that it results from experiences that have nothing to do with them.

But if they still don't like it, I really don't care. I'll never meet them; I rarely know their full names; and I don't even know where in the country they're sitting. But it's *my* life, *my* health, and *my* finances that are at stake if something goes wrong. Nothing comparable is at stake for them.

Of course, my defensive tactics don't stop there. Instead of relying on the insurance company's records, I also make a complete record of every single conversation I have with insurance companies. I write down the date and time of the conversation, the full names (if I can get them) of the people I spoke to, their titles, their departments, their telephone extensions, their geographic locations, and, if possible, the full names of their supervisors. And sometimes I even write a letter to the insurance company memorializing the conversation.

This information can be invaluable if the insurer later tells me that it has no record of any such conversations. Without this information, I end up saying lamely, "I spoke to a woman and she referred me to someone else, and he said . . ." I can almost hear the insurer laughing at me.

With this information, however, I can give answers like: "I spoke with Jean Terrault, in your Brighton, Ohio, office on May 15, at 4:25 P.M. She said she was a customer service representative, and that she reports to John Constantine. Her extension was 5370. She promised that she had made a record of our conversation. Would you check your records again?" Now nobody is laughing.

I'm not saying this is foolproof. It's not. If Jean Terrault is questioned, she probably won't remember me (unless, of course, she found my questions so irritating that she can't forget me—not such a bad thing). I may still be forced to start the entire process again, with an entirely new representative and a new set of reassurances.

But this approach does change the overall dynamic. It gives me some control over the process. It makes the second customer service representative a little concerned about dropping the ball. It makes insurance companies think about complaints to their local insurance departments, about lawsuits, about negligence, and about bad faith. In short, it makes me their problem—which may make them want to solve my problem, just to make me go away.

I've developed a few other tricks for dealing with health insurers. Here's my top ten:

1. MAKE AN ANNUAL INSURANCE FILE

There are many ways to keep track of your insurance records. I've set forth my personal favorite, but feel free to develop your own.

I suggest that every year you take an accordian file and label it "Health Insurance—2001" (or whatever). Then insert file folders for every member of your family, along with one labeled "Policy," one labeled "Miscellaneous" and one labeled "Annual Notebook." Put your policy in the "Policy" folder, your applications and other forms in the "Miscellaneous" folder, and put a fresh legal pad or notebook in the "Annual Notebook" folder (more about that later). The rest of the folders should be empty.

Throughout the year, file away every piece of paper pertaining to your health care. File copies of everything you send in, along with copies of everything your doctors send in (if they'll tell you), along with copies of any responses you receive. Don't be lazy about this; it just takes a minute to staple together a record and drop it into a file. It's well worth your time.

Separate your files by patient, so that you don't have to go through the whole family's records just to find a particular claim. This can be a major time saver. If you receive one letter from your insurance company that lists claims from different family members, make copies and put one in each family member's file. That way, at a moment's notice, you can put your hands on all of the records of anyone whose claims are at issue.

2. MAKE AN ANNUAL NOTEBOOK

Every year, take a clean notebook and use it to keep track of your family's medical care for the year. I would suggest devoting one page to each member of your family. If you do it right, your notes on this page will correspond to the documents that you keep in the file devoted to that family member.

I also suggest using the rest of the notebook to keep track of all discussions you have with your health insurer and, at times, your doctors, laboratories, or other providers. That way, you have all of your notes in one place and you don't have to rummage through your kitchen drawers looking for the backs of the envelopes that you took notes on.

Naturally, you may not always have the notebook with you when you have important conversations. My suggestion is that you try to take the envelopes you wrote on and staple them right into your insurance notebook. It's not a perfect system, but it works.

Assume, for example, that you are using an HMO with an out-of-network option. That means that you will have two types of claims during the year: ones where you pay nothing except limited co-payments, and ones where you pay up front, submitting claims and awaiting reimbursement.

You should be able to keep track, on one sheet of paper, of both types of claims. It's not very hard. On the top of each family member's page in your annual insurance notebook, just make the following columns:

Date of Service	Doctor	Payment	Date of Claim	Deductible	Date of Reimbursement

Throughout the year, make a note of every single medical visit, even if it is not covered (meaning, include things like optometrist checkups and routine dental cleanings). If I know there is no coverage, I write N/C in the last three columns. But you'll still have a record of all uncovered health care for cafeteria-plan purposes, and also for reassessing, at the end of the year, the performance of your health plan.

If the visit is covered under the HMO, note the co-payment in the third column. Then write "N/A" in the remaining three columns. This gives you a quick check, at the end of the year, of how many of the doctors that you used actually participated in the HMO.

If the visit is covered out of network, note in the third column exactly how much you paid. In the fourth column, note the date you submitted the claim. Add to this column every time you resubmit the claim. (This probably could happen several times before most claims are paid. But at least you can tell, at a glance, how many times you've submitted it.)

Until you receive a final response from the insurance company, leave the next two columns blank. Periodically glance over the entire chart to see if there are any blanks that should have been filled in by then. Then call the insurance company to review all of the outstanding claims at once, rather than needing to make multiple phone calls.

Eventually (even if it takes years!) you will receive final responses about all of these claims. As soon as you do, write down the amount reimbursed and the amount assigned to the deductible.

3. KEEP DETAILED RECORDS OF EVERYTHING

In the back of your annual insurance notebook, keep notes of absolutely everything that takes place during the year with your health insurance. This should include notes of every telephone call you make, every person you speak to, and everything they say. This habit will give you some protection against an insurance company or health plan that tends to ignore your calls and requests.

In addition to taking notes it's a good idea to send a letter to your insurance company after every important oral conversation. In your letter, write down exactly what was said to you, by whom, and when. If the comment was *really* important, ask them to write back immediately if you have misstated it in any way. This is an excellent way of making your own record, and not being dependent upon what the insurance company spokesman decided to memorialize about what he or she said.

I also recommend that, once you finally figure out what you think you're owed and why, or what information you need in order to answer a coverage question, write a note to yourself explaining the situation. One of the biggest hurdles to keeping track of your health care is that it often takes months to get anything done. During the time you spend waiting for responses from your insurers, it is all too easy to forget what you were asking for, and why. You can save hours of work if you make clear notes to yourself every step of the way.

4. MAKE AN ACTUAL COPY OF EVERYTHING YOU SEND IN

Sending something to your insurance company can be like tossing it in the trash. It may not arrive in the right office, or be filed in the right place by the right person. It may not be processed, it may not be kept. It certainly may not be paid. The only chance you have is to keep an exact copy of what you sent in.

It's even worthwhile to get copies of everything that other people, like your doctors, send in on your behalf.

Having these copies serves endless purposes. Among other things, it enables you to send duplicate copies to your insurers without much effort. It also enables you to prove that you repeatedly submitted the same materials, which may prove helpful in pursuing an internal grievance, a complaint to a government agency, or even a lawsuit in court.

5. KEEP EVERYTHING THAT YOU RECEIVE

The flip side of keeping copies of your submissions is keeping the originals of everything they send to you.

Everything you receive from your insurance company has potential value. Every letter approving a claim, for example, is evidence of your insurer's fee schedule. It's also evidence of how much you've exhausted of the maximum coverage that you are allowed. Similarly, every EOB assigning a payment to the deductible is evidence that part of your deductible has been exhausted. Also, every EOB denying a claim, or any part of a claim, is evidence of noncovered expenses, for purposes of your cafeteria plan.

Please, please keep all of it. You never know what you'll need to prove, and why. Don't count on your insurance company to find its own copy when the time comes. If the information helps you, but you can't find your copy, don't be surprised if the insurance company can't find its own.

And I really do mean all of it. All too often, people throw out their files, especially once they receive full payment of a claim. Big mistake, especially if you ever expect to see the same doctor again for the same condition. Sometimes, if you get a denial for a doctor visit after previous visits to the same doctor had been fully covered, you can use the proof of previous coverage to show that you are entitled to subsequent coverage. If you have the habit of throwing out these forms, though, you'll have no way of proving anything.

Also, people often err by picking out the parts that they think are important, and throwing away the rest. The problem is that it's impossible to know what will end up important someday. I'd even recommend keeping envelopes—just turn them sideways and staple them along with everything that was inside. That way, if a letter is dated long before the date on the envelope, you'll be able to show—if it ever becomes an issue—when the letter *really* was sent. Remember you never know what issue may someday come up.

6. KEEP CAREFUL TRACK OF YOUR DEDUCTIBLE

One of the best parts of this record-keeping system is that it provides quick information about how much has been assigned to the deductible each year, both by person and by family. I use this information to keep insurers from overcharging our deductibles.

Usually health plans that have any deductibles at all have at least two types: individual deductibles, which are satisfied when an individual's covered expenses exceed a preset amount, and family deductibles, which are satisfied when the covered expenses of a family exceed a larger amount.

Let's say you are a four-person family, with a per-person deductible of $350 and a family deductible of $900. If your seven-year-old daughter breaks her ankle playing soccer, and you seek out-of-network treatment, she's sure to exhaust her $350. If your three-year-old son visits your out-of-network pediatrician as often as he did last year, he'll exhaust his deductible too. That means that you get reimbursement, for the rest of the year, for all of their covered out-of-network expenses.

What about you? You probably rarely go to a doctor for yourself. But when you do, you shouldn't have to meet your full deductible of $350. You should be entitled to reimbursement after just $200 in covered expenses, because your children's expenses will have collectively exhausted $700 of the $900 family deductible.

The problem is that people don't incur medical expenses one at a time. It isn't as though your daughter first exhausts her $350 deductible, then your son exhausts his, and then you head off to the doctor. Instead, your son sees the pediatrician for a bee sting; then you come down with the flu; then your daughter and son both need checkups for camp; then your daughter breaks her wrist; and so on.

Without careful record keeping, it's hard to keep track of individual deductibles—and harder still to keep track of family deductibles. But the system I suggest makes it relatively easy. All you need to do is write down in each family member's "Deductibles" column every payment that your insurer assigns to a deductible. Basic math will tell you when the deductibles have been met.

If you see that your insurer is overcharging your deductible, call them immediately—with your insurance files in your hands. Confirm with them exactly how much they've assigned to deductibles, pulling the actual EOBs from the family member folders and giving them copies if necessary. Secure their agreement to reimburse you the rest. As discussed above, make notes of the conversation in your annual notebook and get as much information as possible about the person who's talking to you.

This system works, and may save you hundreds of dollars a year. I know from personal experience. It seems like every time we receive out-of-network services, our insurers over-charge our deductibles. It has taken months of follow-up at times, but we have recovered many hundreds of dollars in a single year.

7. CHECK EVERYTHING ELSE, TOO

I'm not kidding. If they reject part of your claim, for ex-ample, as above the usual and customary charges, well, maybe it is and maybe it isn't. It certainly is in your insurer's financial interest whenever it says so.

I once received an EOB stating that only $45 was covered of our pediatrician's standard charge of $78 for an office visit. I checked an entire year of EOBs, both before and after the visit in question, and saw that the insurer had always covered the entire $78 charge. I called customer service and received a completely incomprehensible, argumentative explanation, so I proceeded with a written grievance. Within a month, and without any further discussion, a check for the difference came in the mail.

In that particular example, the amount of money at stake may not seem substantial. But it could have been. Here's an-other example.

I once represented a client who had paid a substantial sum to a hospital, without being certain that he owed it. He had paid under protest, after being turned over to a collection agency.

A close review of the hospital and insurance records then showed that his insurer had *also* paid the bill. The hospital had ended up with double recovery without telling anyone—and, on top of it, even had received—and kept—interest from the insurance company for its late payment! In very little time, the hospital agreed to reimburse him the payment, and the interest as well.

Don't be fooled by formal-looking documents that are written in code. Don't assume that they're right and you're wrong. Instead, have confidence in your own abilities and instincts. Whenever you receive a denial, make sure it's right before you accept it. Whenever you receive a bill, make sure you owe it before you pay it.

8. FOLLOW UP EVERY CLAIM

A common problem at insurance companies seems to be ignoring claims. At the end of the year—every single year—I discover that a number of claims simply have been overlooked.

I also discover, each and every year, that all kinds of amazing things have happened to certain claims. For instance, the insurance company has ignored all instructions and paid claims directly to doctors who already have been paid in full. The doctors at times have cashed the checks without telling the patients, and left it to the patients to chase down the money.

Or the insurance company paid claims directly to doctors as requested, but somehow confused the doctors about the reason for the payment. So the doctors accepted the money, assigned it to someone else's account, and then sent the patient's account to a collection agency.

I don't need to tell you, unfortunately, that the list goes on and on. You probably have stories of your own. So be vigilant about your own claims. No one else will.

9. DON'T GET "BALANCE BILLED"

In the new-speak of insurance law, balance billing is when doctors and other providers collect what they can from HMOs, and then bill the patient for the rest. It is a major no-no when you're in a managed care plan. The providers typically have signed contracts stating that they will accept the health plan's fee schedule as full payment, and will not bill the patient at all.

It's easy to detect balance billing when you are on a straight managed care plan. It generally happens whenever you receive a bill from an in-network provider. Unless you intentionally decided to pay for a noncovered service, you are not supposed to be receiving any bills. If you receive one, you should write back immediately, explaining that they have no contractual right to bill you. If you think it's necessary, you may want to send a copy to the HMO and put a "CC" on the letter so that the provider knows you did that. Your problems should stop.

When you are in an HMO with an out-of-network alternative, the detection of balance billing gets much more complicated. The problem is that it can be impossible to tell who is billing you in network and who is billing you out of network.

Hospitals are one of the worst culprits. Assume you are sent to a network hospital by your primary care physician. All's clear for complete coverage. Months later, you receive a bill from one particular department, like radiology. You tell them to talk to your HMO; they respond that they don't participate in your HMO. It turns out that the radiology group is not a part of the hospital—even though it is located in the hospital and uses the hospital's name. So they haven't balance billed you. They're just submitting a bill for out-of-network services that you may be required to pay, then submit to your HMO for reimbursement under the POS option.

You don't have to pay balance bills. You do have to pay out-of-network bills. Don't mix them up, or you'll end up paying bills that never should have been sent to you in the first place.

By the way, someone I know has an interesting system for protecting her family from surprise bills from out-of-network providers, labs, and departments. Whenever she deals with in-network hospitals or providers, she writes a note asking that all referrals be made to in-network providers, labs, and departments, and that she be notified before any out-of-network referrals are made. This approach makes a lot of sense, and you may want to try it.

10. JUST DO IT!

By now, you should be a convert to record keeping. I hope so. Keeping good records is key to your ability to get anywhere with your health insurers and HMOs. The results that you'll see are well worth the little bit of time that's involved.

From TMJ in Arkansas to Toupees in New Hampshire—Know Your Own State's Mandatory-Benefit Laws

Lots of people don't want you to read this chapter.
Maybe not your employer. Certainly not your insurance company.

And possibly not even some of the legislators who passed the laws that you're about to discover.

Here's what they don't want you to know. Each and every one of the fifty states has laws forcing health plans to cover certain medical treatments and services. These "mandatory-benefit" laws apply *no matter what the individual insurance policies say*. These laws affect more than 100 million people in this country, and there is a good chance that you are one of them.

The laws vary wildly. Many states—and now even the federal government—mandate coverage for "mainstream" health issues, such as screening for breast cancer. Others, however, have mandates that are extremely specialized. Ever heard of mandatory "scalp hair prosthesis" coverage (sounds like "toupee" to me)? They've got it in New Hampshire and several other states. How about mandatory port wine stain elimination? If you need it, move to Minnesota. Does hemophilia run in your family? Think New Jersey or Virginia, where you'll have mandatory coverage. Do you have an Alzheimer's problem? Better hope you live in Maryland.

State mandates can mean the difference between life and death. This is certainly true for mandates regarding infertility. These mandates were found in at least 12 states in early 2000; including Arkansas, California, Connecticut, Hawaii, Illinois, Maryland, Massachusetts, New York, Ohio, Rhode Island, Texas, and West Virginia. As a Maryland resident, I know at least seven children (two single births, one set of twins, and one set of triplets) who would not be here if not for the state's mandatory infertility benefits.

Sometimes It Takes a Village To Make a Family*

Elise and Frank Jackson were a young couple with a problem. They suffered from a medical condition that impaired their fertility but was easily correctable by modern technology. The problem was that the technology was expensive, and their health plan did not cover it.

But Elise, a legal secretary, had heard that there might be a state law that could help. So she asked her law firm for assistance, and was referred to the insurance broker who handled the firm's insurance.

That firm's broker quickly took charge. Working through his assistant, Elizabeth Worth, he investigated the laws of Maryland, where Elise and Frank lived, and determined that the state mandates coverage for infertility in certain circumstances.

Worth spoke with, and wrote to, the insurance company about the situation. Her efforts were rewarded with an insurance company letter stating that Elise was entitled to coverage for her infertility. The letter, which was addressed to the broker's office and copied to the law firm, stated simply:

Dear Elizabeth:

As per your request, X Health Plans will cover Elise Jackson's infertility claims because of the following Maryland law:

Section 15-810 Benefits for in vitro fertilization

Covers individuals who reside and work in the State; and is written on an expense-incurred basis. Exclusion of benefits prohibited—A policy, contract, or certificate subject to this section that provides pregnancy-related benefits may not exclude benefits for all outpatient expenses arising from in vitro fertilization.

Please feel free to call me if you have any questions.

Sincerely,
Sr. Account Manager

This short letter opened the door to the future for Elise and Frank. It meant that they were free to proceed with the infertility treatment diagnosed for their medical condition. They did so immediately, deeply grateful for the hard work and assistance of Elise's employer, the employer's broker, the broker's assistant, and even the insurance company representative who precertified the coverage.

But the gratitude that they felt then didn't hold a candle to their emotions nine short months later. At that time, they celebrated the birth of their twin son and daughter.

Hillary Clinton may say it takes a village to raise a child. In this case, it took a village—including a bunch of state legislators in Annapolis, Maryland—to make two.

*While everything in this story really happened, all names have been changed and are completely fictitious.

At the other end of the spectrum, mandated cancer screening can help to avert tragic deaths. Cancer screening, in fact, was the most common mandate by early 2000, with all but one state mandating it in some form. The lone exception was Utah.

Many mandates are not as dramatic; they just help ease the suffering of people with illnesses or conditions. For example, in early 2000 sixteen states had mandates for TMJ, formally known as temporomandibular joint disorder. This disease, which produces jaw pain, typically is excluded from coverage as being dental, rather than medical. The states that gave relief to TMJ sufferers as of 2000 included California, Florida, Georgia, Kentucky, Minnesota, Mississippi, Nevada, New Mexico, North Carolina, North Dakota, Texas, Vermont, Virginia, Washington, West Virginia, and Wisconsin.

Similarly, coverage related to osteoporosis was mandated in at least six states that year: California, Florida, Georgia, Kentucky, Oklahoma, Tennessee, and Texas.

Eight states had mandatory coverage for congenital defects, like cleft lip and cleft palate. They were Colorado, Florida, Indiana, Louisiana, Maryland, Minnesota, North Carolina, and South Carolina.

One state, Minnesota, mandated coverage for Lyme disease, which is excluded under most health plans. Other single-state and double-state mandates were as follows:

Alzheimer's disease	Maryland
antineoplastic therapy drugs	Michigan
attention deficit/hyperactivity disorder	Louisiana
cosmetic or reconstructive surgery after family violence	West Virginia
endometriosis	Kentucky

footwear for disfiguration	California
grandchildren coverage, when children are under 18	Wisconsin
hemophilia	New Jersey Virginia
human leukocyte antigen tests	Rhode Island
inhalers for asthma	Georgia
maxillofacial prosthetic devices	Oregon
ninety-day supply of drugs	Maryland
ovarian cancer monitoring subsequent to treatment	Delaware
port wine stains	Minnesota
prosthesis after laryngectomy	California
sickle-cell anemia	Alabama
Wilm's tumor	New Jersey

For some reason, there seems to be a marked focus among the mandatory-benefit laws on health issues unique to women. Common mandates include pregnancy and childbirth benefits and treatment for breast cancer. Even the federal government has passed mandates focused on women's issues, such as mandatory hospital stays of forty-eight hours following vaginal births and ninety-six hours following cesarean deliveries. (Because of this federal law, these particular mandatory benefits were deleted from the list set forth below.)

Some mandates focus on children, like coverage for newly born children, adopted children, well-child care, and childhood immunizations. Others focus on elder care, such as Alzheimer's disease, osteoporosis, and, to a certain extent, diabetes

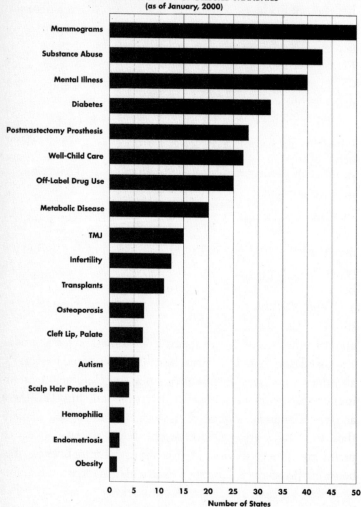

RELATIVE POPULARITY OF SELECTED MANDATES
(as of January, 2000)

Mammograms
Substance Abuse
Mental Illness
Diabetes
Postmastectomy Prosthesis
Well-Child Care
Off-Label Drug Use
Metabolic Disease
TMJ
Infertility
Transplants
Osteoporosis
Cleft Lip, Palate
Autism
Scalp Hair Prosthesis
Hemophilia
Endometriosis
Obesity

0   5   10   15   20   25   30   35   40   45   50
Number of States

coverage. Finally, some apply across the board, such as pharmaceutical benefits.

Political leanings, and unique characteristics, of particular states may be mirrored to a certain extent in their mandatory benefits. For example, the relatively liberal states of Maryland and Minnesota are often identified as having the largest number of state mandates. Another state with lots of mandates is Florida, which has a comparatively large elderly population. California and Texas are up there too, both of which serve as national leaders on issues pertaining to managed care.

In researching this chapter, I reviewed summaries of the principal mandatory-benefits laws compiled by organizations like the National Association of Insurance Commissioners and the National Conference of State Legislatures. I also reviewed the actual laws of the fifty states, and contacted all fifty insurance departments.

Now, stop and think for a minute. Your state has laws that may force your health plan to provide certain benefits to you, no matter what your policy says. If you're like most people, I'll bet you didn't know about this.

That's no accident. Almost every player in the health insurance arena has a reason why they don't want you to know about these laws.

Your health plan may be the prime culprit. Your plan probably does not want you to get any more coverage than it promised to provide (and maybe not that much, but that's for another chapter). Among other things, it may not have taken these mandates into account when it calculated your annual premium. Even if it had, the coverage you actually need may be so expensive that it outweighs what you paid.

Another culprit may be your employer. A prime reason behind the boom in managed care is the desire to reduce health insurance premiums. Employers keep their premiums low by keeping health care costs down. They may not want you to know about mandatory-benefit laws that give you the right to demand additional benefits. At least theoretically, those same benefits could drive up next year's premium.

Ironically, even the state legislators who passed these mandatory-benefit laws may have difficulty educating the public about them. These laws often contain many technical twists and turns. As a result, it can be difficult to explain them accurately, to enforce them, and to teach people to enforce them for themselves.

For example, insurance companies and health plans typically are not required to make their plans match the state laws. For example, your plan may state that it completely excludes infertility coverage. Your state, however, may mandate coverage for certain types of infertility treatments. It is perfectly okay, under existing laws, for your plan not to tell you about this and even to state the opposite.

Sometimes, states police their mandates strictly. For example, in late 1998 the Maryland Insurance Administration fined one insurer tens of thousands of dollars for failing to comply with a state law requiring managed care companies to provide members with supplies of at least ninety days of "maintenance drugs" for chronic conditions such as high blood pressure. But other times, states are slow when it comes to enforcement.

So—what's a policyholder to do?

Two things. First, find out what benefits are mandatory in your state. Second, make your health plan give these benefits to you.

Your first job is easy. In fact, it's done. The majority of the mandatory-benefit laws of all fifty states—at least as of early 2000—are set forth at the end of this chapter. State by state, in alphabetical order, you will find a brief description of most of the laws that were in effect when this book went to press, and even their statute numbers.

Your second job is a bit harder. To make your insurer comply with the mandatory-benefit laws, try following these ten steps:

1. Identify the type of benefit you hope to receive.

2. Read your plan and see if it's covered.

3. If not, look up your state's laws in this chapter. If you find the benefit you want, write down the statute number.

4. Call your insurance company and ask them if they provide this type of coverage.

5. If they say no, tell them you've heard this benefit is mandatory in your state. *Don't* say anything more at this stage—sometimes less information gets you further, faster. But if they question you, then go ahead and give them the statute numbers.

6. At this point, they should give you the benefit. But if not, go on to steps 7–10.

7. If they still deny the benefit, ask for a detailed explanation of the basis for the denial in writing. Get the name, title, office location and extension of every person who denies it orally, and note the date and time of the telephone calls. Unless you get this information, you may be told later that these conversations never happened. (See Step Eight.)

8. Reach out to third parties like the insurance commissioner, the attorney general, and the Department of Health in your state. The names and addresses of the fifty insurance commissioners as of 2000 are set forth in Appendix B, and the names and addresses of the fifty attorney generals as of 2000 are set forth in Appendix C.

Tell them what you think you're entitled to, and why, and what your insurer has told you. Ask them how you should proceed, and whether you're really entitled to the benefit you're seeking. If they think you're off base, consider saving your energy for a different fight.

9. Don't stop with the government. Many consumer organization are out there that may help you or may be able to point you toward an organization that can do so. Lists of the names and addresses of some consumer-oriented organizations are set forth in Appendix D.

10. Appeal the denial through the ordinary appeals procedure followed by your plan. Learn all the deadlines right from the start, so you don't get caught in one of these administrative sandtraps. At this point, let your insurance company know about all the third parties that you have contacted for help.

The key to getting coverage that is mandated by your state is letting your health plan know *you* know the law. If you don't say anything, they'll try to enforce the terms of the plan. If you tell them about the law, though, they usually surrender quickly.

As a Maryland resident (remember, that's the state with the most mandatory-benefit laws), I've seen this happen first-hand. For example, when I was pregnant with one of my children, my insurer at the time paid for only twenty-four hours in the hospital following the birth. I knew that, at that time, Maryland mandated a forty-eight-hour hospital stay. (The federal government did not yet do so.)

When I called my insurer for precertification, as required by the plan, I asked how much time I was precertified to receive. The customer service representative said twenty-four hours. I then told her I lived in Maryland. (My law firm's health plan covered a number of states, so she would not necessarily know this unless I said so.) She paused, then asked me to wait on hold. After about ten minutes, she returned with the news that I now was precertified for forty-eight hours.

That's often how it works. It can be easy. And depending on the coverage at issue, it may help create, or change, or save, somebody's life.

For a few important reasons, though, you still cannot treat this summary of the state laws as the gospel. First of all, if you think insurance policies are hard to read, you should try reading actual laws. They are usually filled with all kinds of limitations, conditions, technicalities, and red tape. As a result, it is impossible to explain here, or in any other general summary, the *exact* requirements of each and every mandate of each of the fifty states.

I have tried simply to identify—in plain English—the subject matter of the states' mandates. In many cases, that information should be all you need to get the mandated coverage. If your insurer questions the existence of the statute, give it the statute numbers that are set forth here. If the mandate really applies to your situation, that should do the trick.

If it doesn't, however, and the issue is important enough, you may need to contact a lawyer. Show him or her this list, along with the statute numbers. If nothing else, you may save a few minutes of expensive research time.

The following statute regarding in vitro fertilization, which was in effect in Maryland in 2000, is an example of an actual mandatory-benefit law—and a good example of why, in certain circumstances, you will need a lawyer:

Section 15-810. In Vitro Fertilization

(a) This section applies to:

(1) each individual hospital or major medical insurance policy of an insurer that:

(i) 1. is delivered or issued for delivery in the State; or 2. covers individuals who reside and work in the State; or

(ii) is written on an expense-incurred basis;

(2) each group or blanket health insurance policy of an insurer that:

(i) 1. is issued or delivered in the State; or 2. covers individuals who reside and work in the State; and

(ii) is written on an expense-incurred basis; and

(3) each individual or group medical or major medical contract or certificate of a nonprofit health service plan that:

(i) is issued or delivered in the State; or

(ii) covers individuals who reside and work in the State.

(b) (1) A policy, contract, or certificate subject to this section that provides pregnancy-related benefits may not exclude benefits for all outpatient expenses arising from in vitro fertilization procedures performed on the policyholder, subscriber, or certificate holder, or dependent spouse of the policyholder, subscriber, or certificate holder.

(2) The benefits under this subsection shall be provided to the same extent as the benefits provided for other pregnancy-related procedures [emphasis supplied].

(c) Subsection (b) of this section applies if:

(1) the patient is the policyholder, subscriber, or certificate holder, or a covered dependent of the policyholder, subscriber, or certificate holder;

(2) the patient's oocytes are fertilized with the patient's spouse's sperm;

(3) (i) the patient and the patient's spouse have a history of infertility of at least 5 years' duration; or (ii) the infertility is associated with any of the following medical conditions: 1. endometriosis; 2. exposure in utero to diethylstilbestrol, commonly known as DES; or 3. blockage of, or surgical removal of, one or both fallopian tubes (lateral or bilateral salpingectomy);

(4) the patient has been unable to attain a successful pregnancy through a less costly infertility treatment for which coverage is available under the policy, contract, or certificate; and

(5) the in vitro fertilization procedures are performed at medical facilities that conform to the American College of Obstetricians and Gynecologists guidelines for in vitro fertilization clinics or to the American Fertility Society minimal standards for programs of in vitro fertilization.

The italicized section is the one that actually mandates coverage for in vitro fertilization. The other sections basically set limits on when it applies.

A second reason why you cannot treat this summary of state mandates, or any other summary, as the gospel is that these mandates change periodically. The good news is that mandates usually are added, not deleted. For example, only one state—Hawaii—mandated coverage for contraceptive services in 1998. The next year the list tripled, with the additions of Georgia and Maryland. In 2000, the list increased again.

The summary here will tell you the great majority of the mandates that were in effect as of the publication date. If you are interested in a particular mandate, though, and you do not see it here, don't give up immediately. There's a chance that this mandate may have been added by your state since this book went to press, or for some other reason was not included here.

There's also a chance that your state may have passed a different type of law—a "patient protection"—that is outside the scope of this chapter, but that still may be helpful to you. Such patient protections include: (1) requirements that health plans pay for services provided by any provider willing to abide by the terms of the health plans; (2) requirements that health plans cover any emergency services that a "prudent layperson" reasonably thought were necessary; (3) requirements that health plans disclose how to obtain nonformulary prescription drugs; (4) requirements that health plans permit women direct access to OB/GYNs; and (5) requirements to secure continuity of care when a provider leaves a plan.

One way to get up-to-the-minute information about your state's mandatory-benefit laws, and about its patient protection laws as well, is to check the Web site of your state department of insurance. Many of them set forth all state regulations on insurance, and you should be able to find out whatever you need. If you're looking for an update on a mandate set forth here, use the section number that follows each and every mandate as a guide. These section numbers identify exactly where the mandates could be found as of the publication date.

If you don't use the Internet, or you can't find the insurance laws for your state there, you also can try calling your state insurance department for help, or of course a private attorney. The addresses and phone numbers of all fifty state insurance departments are set forth here in Appendix B. Tell the insurance department the type of health plan that you have, the subject matter of the mandate that you're interested in, and—if necessary—the statute number that is listed in the attached summary. I have made similar requests of the departments of all fifty states, and have found most of them to be remarkably cooperative. Many of them even sent me hard copies of the insurance laws that they believed would answer my questions.

A third reason why you can't treat this summary as the gospel is that it does not attempt to include every type of mandate that may exist in every state. Instead it sets forth only the mandates that I think are of principal interest: usually the ones that require coverage for particular illnesses and conditions. I have not attempted to include each and every mandate, such as mandates that newly born children be covered automatically from the moment that they are born, and mandates that all services performed in outpatient departments or other facilities outside of hospitals be given the same coverage as inpatient services in hospitals. All you need to know about such mandates right now is that most states have some.

A fourth caveat is that, even when a state mandates coverage, the mandate may not apply to every type of health plan and insurance company. Sometimes, mandates apply only to HMOs; sometimes only to group plans; and so on. I've tried to set forth the mandates and all the relevant statute numbers, which should be all you need to get the mandated coverage. If your insurer responds that this mandate does not apply to your plan, you may at that point need to check with a lawyer.

Also, while these mandates apply to more than 100 million people, they still do not apply to everyone. In particular, they do not apply to the minority of people who are insured through private employers, and whose employers fully "self-fund" their health plans. The reasons are many, complex, and, some say, ludicrous.

All you really need to know about this opaque topic is whether or not you are part of the minority who don't get the benefit of these laws. The easiest way to find out is to ask your employer. The exact question you should ask is: "Is our health plan fully self-funded under ERISA?"

Don't accept an answer like, "Yes, we do fall under ERISA." That, alone, means nothing. *All* health plans offered by private employers fall under ERISA; that's one of the things the act does. Find out whether your particular health plan is fully self-funded. If it is, the state mandatory-benefit laws may not apply. If it is not, though, these laws should protect you.

Depending on the dynamic in your company, you may not want to share with your employer the details behind your question. Employers may not be thrilled when employees seek expensive coverage that could provoke an increase in the next year's premium. The law in this area is so complicated, however, that some employers may not necessarily realize why you are asking the question.

All that said, let's get down to it. Here they are—the great majority of the mandatory-benefit laws for each of the fifty states, as of 2000:

ALABAMA

Mandatory coverage for mammograms on the following schedule: women ages 40–49, at least every 2 years; ages 50 and over, every year; both subject to more frequent screening on recommendation of physician (Sec. 27-50-4).

At least 30 days of inpatient treatment for alcoholism per year, or an equivalent amount of time in a short-term residential treatment facility or on an outpatient basis. Equivalency formula is mandated by the state (Sec. 27-20A-4).

No exclusion for a drug on the grounds that it is being used for other purposes than approved by the Food and Drug Administration, if the drug treatment is recognized in at least one standard reference compendium. This mandate does not require insurers to provide coverage for any experimental or investigational drug that the FDA has found to be contraindicated for treatment of a condition (Sec. 27-1-10.1).

Treatment or care of sickle-cell anemia, in accordance with other policy provisions (Sec. 27-5-13).

ALASKA

Baseline mammograms for women ages 35–39, mammograms every 2 years for women ages 40–49, and mammograms every year for women age 50 and over. Mammograms shall be covered at any age when there is a family history of breast cancer, upon referral of physician. Coverage shall be no less favorable than other radiological exams (Sec. 21.42.375).

Annual prostate screening for men age 40–49 in high-risk group, meaning a man who is African-American or has a family history of prostate cancer; and annual prostate screening for all men 50 or older (Sec. 21.42.395).

Annual Pap smears for women 18 or older (Sec. 21.42.395).

Treatment of alcohol and drug abuse at least to specified minimums (Sec. 21.42.365).

Formulas necessary for the treatment of phenylketonuria (Sec. 21.42.380).

Offer of dental, vision and hearing coverage (Sec. 21.42.385).

ARIZONA

Baseline mammograms for women ages 35–39; mammograms every 2 years for women ages 40–49; and mammograms every year for women age 50 and over (Secs. 20-826(I); 20-934(G); 20-1057(J); 20-1342(A)(10); 20-1402(A)(6); 20-1404(H)

Breast reconstruction and at least 2 external postoperative prostheses for insurers that cover mastectomies (Secs. 20-826(H); 20-934(F); 20-1057(I); 20-1342(A)(9); 20-1402(A)(5); 20-1404(G).

Equipment and supplies that are medically necessary for the management of diabetes, including blood glucose monitors, test strips, and syringes (Secs. 20-826(P); 20-934(L); 20-1057(T); 20-1342(D); 20-1402(D); 20-1404(M); 20-2325).

ARKANSAS

Baseline mammograms for women ages 35–40; mammograms every 2 years for women ages 40–49; mammograms every year for women age 50 and over; and mammograms without regard to age, based on recommendations of a physician (Sec. 23-79-140).

Breast reconstruction and prosthetic devices for insurers that cover mastectomies. (Sec. 23-94-405).

Routine periodic physical examinations to age 18, to at least specified minimum benefit levels (Sec. 23-79-141).

In vitro fertilization to specified minimum and maximum benefit levels (Secs. 23-85-137; 23-86-118).

Mental health and developmental disorders under the same terms and conditions as treatment for other medical illness and conditions (Sec. 23-99-506).

Alcohol and drug abuse to specified minimum levels (Sec. 23-79-139).

Equipment, supplies, services, and education for treatment and management of diabetes (Secs. 23-79-602 and 23-79-603).

Drugs used to treat cancers of a different type than approved by the FDA if recommended in medical literature (Sec. 23-79-147).

Offer of coverage for loss or impairment of speech or hearing. (Sec. 23-79-130).

Testing of newborn infants for PKU and of non-Caucasian infants for sickle-cell anemia, among other diseases. (Sec. 23-79-129).

CALIFORNIA

Baseline mammograms for women ages 35–39; mammograms every 2 years for women ages 40–49; and mammograms every year for women age 50 and over (Secs. 1367.65; 10123.81).

Annual Pap smears for women over 18 (Secs. 1367.66; 10123.18; 11512.55).

Prostate cancer screening when medically necessary and consistent with good professional practices (Secs. 1367.64; 10123.83).

Physical examinations to age 16, consistent with the recommendations of the American Academy of Pediatrics, and must offer such coverage for ages 17–18 (Secs. 1367.3; 1367.35; 10123.5; 10123.55).

Offer of coverage for infertility treatment other than in vitro fertilization (Secs. 1374.55; 10119.6; 11512.28).

Coverage for severe mental disorders. (Sec. 1374.72). Also, all group contracts must offer coverage for the following disorders of the brain in the same manner as physical illnesses: schizophrenia, schizo-affective disorder, bipolar disorder, or delusional depression; and pervasive developmental disorder (Secs. 10123.15; 10125).

Prosthesis or reconstructive surgery to restore symmetry incident to mastectomy (Secs. 1367.6; 10123.8).

Self-management education programs for diabetes (Secs. 1367.5; 1367.51; 10176.6; 10177.7).

Prosthetic devices to restore a method of speaking for people who have undergone laryngectomies, when contract covered the surgery (Secs. 1367.61; 10123.82).

Offer of coverage for alcohol or substance abuse (Secs. 1367.2; 10123.6; 11512.14).

Offer of coverage for special footwear for person who suffer from foot disfigurement (Secs. 1367.19; 10123.141; 11512.178).

Prescription contraceptive drugs if plan provides drug coverage, except in specialized circumstances (Sec. 1367.25).

No exclusion of a drug on the grounds that it is being used for other purposes than approved by the Food and Drug Administration, if the drug treatment is recognized in at least one standard reference compendium. This mandate does not require insurers to provide coverage for any experimental or investigational drug that the FDA has found to be contraindicated for treatment of a condition (Secs. 1367.21; 10123.195; 11512.182).

Services related to the diagnosis, treatment, and management of osteoporosis (Secs. 1367.67; 10123.185; 11512.24)

Surgical procedures directly affecting the upper or lower jaw-bone, or associated with bone joints, if medically necessary (Secs. 1367.68; 10123.21).

Offer of coverage for acupuncture (Sec. 1373.10).

No requirement of face-to-face contact between a provider and a patient for services appropriately provided through telemedicine (Secs. 1367.13; 10123.85).

Anesthesia and hospitalization for dental procedures for patients under seven and in other specified circumstances (Secs. 1374.71; 10119.9).

No requirement of prior authorization for ambulance services provided through the 911 emergency response system (Secs. 1371.5; 10126.6).

COLORADO

Baseline mammograms for women ages 35–39; mammograms every 2 years for women ages 40–49 or yearly for women in high-risk categories; and mammograms every year for women ages 50–65. Maximum coverage amount is fixed by statute, with amount to be adjusted according to the Consumer Price Index (Sec. 10-16-104(4)).

Prostate cancer screening (Sec. 10-16-104(10)).

Correction of, or treatment for, cleft lip or cleft palate or both, in newborn children (Sec. 10-16-104(1)).

Mental illness, with specified minimum benefits. Biologically based mental illness is to be covered comparably to other types of physical illness. Mental illnesses that are to be covered include schizophrenia, schizo-affective disorder, major depressive disorder, bipolar disorder, obsessive-compulsive disorder, panic disorder, and pervasive developmental disorder or autism (Secs. 10-16-104(5); 10-16-104(5.5)).

Treatment for alcohol abuse, to at least a specified minimum (Sec. 10-16-104(9)).

Equipment, supplies, and outpatient self-management training and education, including medical nutrition therapy, for diabetes (Sec. 10-16-104(13)).

Anesthesia and hospitalization services for dental procedures for dependent children and certain other situations (Sec. 10-16-104(12).

Home health services and hospice care (Sec. 10-16-104(8)).

Prosthetic devices (Sec. 10-16-104(14)).

CONNECTICUT

Baseline mammograms for women ages 35–39; mammograms every 2 years for women ages 40–49; and mammograms every year for women age 50 and over (Sec. 38a-503 (indiv); Sec. 38a-530 (group)).

Preventive pediatric care consistent with coverage provided for other services, through age 6 (Sec. 38a-535).

Offer of coverage for necessary treatments for infertility, including in vitro fertilization procedures (Sec. 38a-536).

Mental or nervous conditions, with specified minimum benefits. Biologically based mental illness is to be covered comparably to medical and surgical conditions. Mental illnesses that are to be covered include schizophrenia, schizo-affective disorder, major depressive disorder, bipolar disorder, obsessive-compulsive disorder, panic disorder, and pervasive developmental disorder or autism (Secs. 38a-488a; 38a-514).

Low-protein modified food products intended for the dietary treatment of inherited metabolic disease if administered under the direction of a physician (Sec. 38a-518c)

Treatment of leukemia, including outpatient chemotherapy, and reconstructive surgery or prosthesis following mastectomy. Coverage must include reconstructive surgery on breast on which mastectomy was performed and reconstructive surgery on nondiseased breast to produce a symmetrical appearance (Secs. 38a-504; 38a-542).

Treatment of alcohol abuse or medical complications thereof (Sec. 38a-533; 38a-539).

Laboratory and diagnostic tests for diabetes, including medically necessary equipment (Sec. 38a-518d)

Drugs used to treat cancers of a different type than approved by FDA, if recommended in medical literature (Secs. 38a-492b (indiv.) and 38a-518b (group)).

Offer of rehabilitation services (Sec. 38a-523).

Home health care (Secs. 38a-493; 38a-520).

Chiropractic services (Sec. 38a-534).

Occupational therapy (Secs. 38a-496; 38a-524).

No requirement of preauthorization before calling 911 if a person believes that there is an emergency that threatens life or limb in such a manner that a need for immediate medical care is created to prevent death or serious impairment of health (Secs. 38a-498a; 38a-525a).

No requirement for a person to obtain prescription drugs only from a mail-order pharmacy (Sec. 38a-544).

DELAWARE

Baseline mammograms at age 35; mammograms every 2 years from 40–50; mammograms every year over age 50; and mammograms as ordered by physicians for women in high-risk categories. The benefit should not exceed the least expensive charge in the area (Sec. 3552(c)).

Annual Pap smears (Sec. 3552(a)).

Annual screening for prostate cancer (Sec. 3552(b)).

Treatment for serious mental illness, comparable to the coverage given to other illnesses. Mental illnesses that are to be covered include schizophrenia, bipolar disorder and anorexia nervosa (Title 18, Secs. 3343 and 3566).

Baseline lead poisoning screening tests at or around 12 months of age, or younger for children at high-risk for lead poisoning (Sec. 3554).

CA-125 monitoring of ovarian cancer subsequent to treatment (Sec. 3555).

Child immunizations (Sec. 3558).

DISTRICT OF COLUMBIA

Baseline mammograms and annual screenings (Sec. 35-2402).

Annual Pap smears (Sec. 35-2402).

Preventive care services, with unlimited visits to age 12 and three visits per year for ages 12–18 (Sec. 35-1102).

Mental illness, with at least specified minimum benefits (Secs. 35-2301 and 35-2311).

Treatment of drug and alcohol abuse, with at least specified minimum benefits (Secs. 35-2301 to 35-2311).

No denial of emergency care on grounds of lack of prior authorization (Sec. 35-4802).

FLORIDA

Baseline mammograms for women ages 35–39; mammograms every 2 years for women ages 40–49; and mammograms every year for women age 50 and over. Group and individual contracts must offer this coverage without deductibles or coinsurance (Secs. 627.6418; 627.6613).

Treatment of cleft lip and cleft palate in children under the age of 18 (Secs. 627.64193; 627.66911; 641.31).

Treatment for mental and nervous disorders to levels specified (Sec. 627.668).

Prescription and nonprescription enteral formulas for treatment of diseases of malabsorption (Sec. 627.42395).

Offer of coverage for prosthetic devices and breast reconstructive surgery incident to a mastectomy, including to reestablish symmetry between the two breasts (Secs. 627.6417; 627.6612; 641.31(32)).

Treatment for substance abuse (Sec. 627.669).

Medically appropriate and necessary equipment, supplies, and outpatient self-management training and educational services used to treat diabetes (Secs. 627.6408; 627.65745; 641.31(26)).

Drugs used to treat cancers of a different type than approved by the FDA, if recommended in medical literature (Sec. 627.4239).

Diagnosis and treatment of osteoporosis for high-risk individuals (Secs. 627.6409; 627.6691; 641.31(27)).

No exclusion for diagnosis or surgical procedures on bones and joints of jaw and face (Secs. 627.65735; 641.31094).

No exclusion for bone marrow transplants following ablative therapy with curative intent (Sec. 627.4236).

Anesthesia and hospitalization services for dental procedures for children under 8, and in certain other situations (Secs. 627.65755; 641.31(34)).

No requirement of prior authorization for prehospital transport or treatment, or for emergency services and care (Sec. 641.513).

GEORGIA

Baseline mammograms for women ages 35–39; mammograms every 2 years for women ages 40–49; and mammograms every year for women age 50 and over; or any schedule ordered by a physician for women in high-risk categories (Secs. 33-29-3.2; 33-30-4.2).

Annual Pap smears (Secs. 33-29-3.2; 33-30-4.2).

Annual prostate cancer screening for men age 45 or over, or age 40 and over when ordered by physician (Secs. 33-29-3.2; 33-30-4.2).

Periodic review of child's physical and emotional status, including immunizations, from birth through age 5, exempt from deductibles (Secs. 33-30-4.5; 33-29-3.4).

Treatment of mental disorders to the same extent as treatment for physical illnesses (Secs. 33-24-28.1; 33-24-29).

No exclusion for treatment of temporomandibular joint disorders (Secs. 33-29-20; 33-30-14).

Offer of coverage for medically necessary equipment, supplies, pharmacological agents, and outpatient self-therapy for diabetes as prescribed by physicians (Sec. 33-34-59.2).

Offer of coverage for bone mass measurement for prevention, diagnosis, and treatment of osteoporosis (Secs. 31-15A-2 to 31-15A-3).

Offer of coverage for heart transplants, at the same levels as for other physical illnesses (Secs. 33-29-3.1; 33-30-4.1).

Offer of coverage for bone marrow transplants for treatment of breast cancer and Hodgkin's disease (Secs. 33-29-3.3; 33-30-4.4).

Annual chlamydia screening test for venereal disease for covered women ages 29 or less (Sec. 31-17-4.1).

Option of offering coverage for treatment of morbid obesity (Sec. 33-24-59.1).

Coverage for any contraceptive drug approved by the FDA, if contract or policy covers prescription drugs (Sec. 33-24-59.6).

No exclusion for prescription inhalers for asthma ordered by physicians, if contract or policy covers prescription drugs (Sec. 33-24-59.8).

Anesthesia and hospitalization services for dental procedures for dependent children, and in certain other situations (Sec. 33-24-1).

No exclusion for use of drugs in manner different than approved by FDA, if recommended in at least one standard reference compendium (Sec. 33-53-2).

HAWAII

Baseline mammograms for women ages 35–39; mammograms every 2 years for women ages 40–49; mammograms every year for women age 50 and over; and mammograms at any age on the recommendation of a physician (Secs. 431:10A-116; 432D-23).

Health supervision services, exempt from deductibles, through age 5 (Secs. 3431:10A-115.5; 431:10A-206.5).

Congenital defects and birth abnormalities in newly born children (Secs. 431:10A-115; 432D-23).

One-time only benefit for outpatient in vitro fertilization expenses, based on certain conditions (Secs. 431:10A-116.5; 432D-23).

Treatment of mental illness with at least specified minimum benefits, including outpatient treatment (Secs. 431M-2 to 431 M-7; 432D-23).

Treatment of alcohol and drug dependency to at least specified minimums, including outpatient treatment (Secs. 431M-2 to 431M-7; 432D-23).

All group contracts that cover pregnancy-related services must provide, at employer's option, contraceptive services (Sec. 431: 10A-116.6; 431:10A-116.7; 432D-23).

Coverage for emergency services, 24 hours a day and 7 days a week, without regard to whether a member obtained prior authorization for these services (Secs. 431:10A-101).

No requirement of face-to-face contact between a provider and a patient for services appropriately provided through telemedicine (Sec. 431:10A-116.3).

Coverage of hospice care at specified minimums, for contracts that provide hospice coverage (Sec. 431:10A-119).

Medical foods and low-protein modified food products (Sec. 431: 10A-120).

IDAHO

Baseline mammograms for women ages 35–39; mammograms every 2 years for women ages 40–49; mammograms every year for women age 50 and over; and any woman desiring one for a medical cause (Secs. 41-2144, 41-2218, 41-3441, 41-3926).

ILLINOIS

Baseline mammograms for women ages 35–39; mammograms every 1 to 2 years for women ages 40–49; and mammograms every year for women age 50 and over (Secs. 5/356g; 125/4-6.1).

Annual cervical smears or Pap smears for women (Sec. 5/356u).

Annual digital rectal examination and prostate-specific antigen tests upon recommendation of physicians for asymptomatic men 50 and over, African-American men 40 and over, and men 40 and over with a family history of prostate cancer (Secs. 5/356u; 125/4-6.5).

Colorectal cancer screening with sigmoidoscopy or fecal occult blood testing once every 3 years for persons age 50 or over, or for younger persons who are classified as high risk (Secs. 5/356x; 125/5-3).

Infertility expenses, including in vitro fertilization (Sec. 5/356m).

Prosthetic devices or reconstructive surgery incidental to mastectomies (Secs. 5/356g; 5/356t).

No exclusion for treatment of alcoholism (Sec. 5/367).

Training and education on diabetes self-management, equipment, and supplies (Secs. 5/365w; 125/5-3).

No exclusions for removal of breast implants when the removal is medically necessary for the treatment of sickness or injury, except if the implants were implanted solely for cosmetic reasons (Secs. 5/356p; 125/4-6.2).

No exclusion for use of drugs for treatment of cancer in manner different than approved by FDA, if recommended in at least one standard reference compendium (Sec. 125/4-6.3).

Offer of coverage for experimental cancer treatments for persons with terminal conditions. (Sec. 5/356y).

INDIANA

Baseline mammograms for women ages 35–39, mammograms every 2 years for women ages 40–49, and mammograms every year for women age 50 and over (Secs. 5-10-8-7.2; 27-8-14-6; 27-13-17-15.3).

Prostate cancer screening for men age 40 and over in high risk category and for all men age 50 and over (Sec. 27-8-14.7-4).

Treatment of cleft lip and cleft palate for newly born children (Sec. 27-8-5.6-2).

No exclusion for a drug on grounds that the drug is being used for other purposes than approved by the FDA if the drug treatment is recognized in at least one standard reference compendium (Secs. 27-8-20-7).

Equipment, supplies, and self-management training for the treatment of diabetes (Sec. 27-8-14.5).

Prosthetic devices and reconstructive breast surgery to produce symmetry subsequent to mastectomy (Secs. 27-8-5-26; 27-13-7-14).

Colorectal cancer screening (Sec. 27-8-14.8-3).

Anesthesia and hospitalization charges for dental procedures if warranted by the insured's mental or physical condition (Sec. 27-8-5-27).

Offer of coverage for nonexperimental surgical treatment of morbid obesity (Sec. 27-8-14.1-4).

IOWA

Baseline mammograms for women ages 35–39, mammograms every 2 years for women ages 40–49, and mammograms every year for women age 50 and over (Sec. 514C.4).

No contract that covers prescription drugs may require a person to obtain them only from a mail-order pharmacy, provided that the person can obtain the drugs from a pharmacy willing to meet the same terms and conditions (Sec. 514c.5).

Equipment, supplies, and self-management training and education programs for the treatment of diabetes (Sec. 514c.18).

KANSAS

Coverage for mammograms performed at direction of doctor (Secs. 40-2,229 to 2,230).

Coverage for Pap smears performed at direction of doctor (Secs. 40-2,229 to 2,230).

Prostate cancer screening for men age 40 and over in high-risk category and for all men age 50 and over (Sec. 40-2,164).

No exclusion of a prescription drug for cancer on grounds that the drug is being used for other purposes than approved by the FDA if the drug treatment is recognized in at least one standard reference compendium (Sec. 40-2,168).

Prosthesis and reconstruction of breast following mastectomy (Sec. 40-2,166)

Immunizations to age 5 (Sec. 40-2,102).

Treatment of mental or nervous conditions with at least specified minimum benefits (Sec. 40-2,105).

Equipment, supplies, and self-management training and education in the treatment of diabetes (Sec. 40-2,163).

Treatment of alcohol and drug abuse to specified limits (Sec. 40-2,105).

Anesthesia and hospitalization for dental care for persons 5 and under, and in other specified circumstances (Sec. 40-2,165).

No requirement of prior authorization for emergency services if symptoms indicate that an emergency medical condition exists (Sec. 40-4,603).

KENTUCKY

Baseline mammograms for women ages 35–39 and mammograms every year for women age 40 and over. Contracts may limit coverage to $50 per screening (Secs. 304.17-316; 304.18-098; 304.32-1591; 304.38-1935).

Offer of coverage for mental illness that is at least what is offered for physical illness (Secs. 304.17-318; 304.18-036; 304.32-165; 304-38-193).

Offer of coverage that includes all stages of breast reconstruction surgery following mastectomies that result from breast cancer (Secs. 304.17-3165; 304.17A-134; 304.18-0983; 304.32-1593; 304.38-1934).

Offer of coverage for bone density testing for women 35 and older (Secs. 304.17-3163; 304.17A-134; 304.18-0983; 304.32-1593; 304.38-1934).

Offer of coverage for the diagnosis and treatment of endometriosis (Secs. 304.17-3163; 304.17A-134; 304.18-0983; 304.32-1593; 304.38-1934).

Offer of coverage for alcohol abuse of at least a specified minimum (Secs. 304.18-130 to 304.18-180).

Treatment of temporomandibular and craniomandibular disease. (Secs. 304.17-319; 304.18-0365; 304.32-1585; 304.38-1937).

Coverage for treatment of autism for children ages 2–21, up to a $500 maximum per month (Sec. 304.17A-143).

Equipment, supplies, and outpatient self-management training and education for the treatment of diabetes (Sec. 304.17A-148).

Cochlear implants for persons with profound hearing impairment (Sec. 304.17A-131).

Drugs used to treat cancers of a different type than approved by FDA if recommended in medical literature (Sec. 304.17A-137).

High-dose chemotherapy and autologous bone marrow transplant as treatment for breast cancer that has progressed to metastatic disease, with same coinsurance and deductibles as for other procedures (Secs. 304.17-3165; 304.17A-135; 304.18-0985; 304.32-1595; 304.38-1936).

LOUISIANA

Baseline mammograms for women ages 35–39; mammograms every 2 years for women ages 40–49, or more frequently if recommended by a physician; and mammograms every year for women age 50 and over (Sec. 215.11).

Annual Pap smears (Sec. 215.11).

Prostate cancer screening for men age 40 and over as medically necessary, and for all men age 50 and over. Mandate applies to contracts issued on or after 1/1/98 (Sec. 215.11).

Treatment of cleft palate, including related needs such as orthodontics and speech therapy (Sec. 22:215.8).

Immunizations to age 6 (Sec. 22:215:14).

An option to purchase coverage for mental and nervous disorders that is the same as for physical illness (Sec. 22:669).

Reconstruction of the breast on which the surgery was performed and reconstruction of the other breast to produce a symmetrical appearance (Sec. 22:215.22).

Treatment of alcoholism and drug abuse (Sec. 22:215.5).

Diagnosis and treatment of attention deficit/hyperactivity disorder (Sec. 22:215.15).

Equipment, supplies, and outpatient self-management training for diabetes (Sec. 22:215.21).

An interpreter for medical treatment for hearing-impaired persons (Sec. 22:215.10).

Drugs used to treat cancers of a different type than approved by FDA if recommended in medical literature (Sec. 215.20).

Offer of coverage for rehabilitative physical therapy, occupational therapy, and speech and language pathology therapy (Sec. 22:230.1).

Anesthesia and hospitalization charges for dental procedures if warranted by the insured's mental or physical condition (Secs. 22:228.7(A); 22:230.3).

Coverage for clinical trials for cancer under specified circumstances (Sec. 22:230.4).

MAINE

Mammograms at least once a year for women age 40 and over. The benefits must be at the same level as other radiological procedures, with no specific deductibles (Tit. 24-A Sec. 2320-A; 24-A Sec. 2745-A; 24-A Sec. 2837-A; 24-A Sec. 4237-A).

Pap smears, if recommended by a physician (Tit. 24-A Sec. 2320-E).

Screenings for early detection of prostate cancer once a year for men age 50–72 (Tit. 24 Sec 2325-C; 24-A Sec. 2745-G; 24-A Sec. 2837-H; 24-A Sec. 4244).

Treatment of mental illness, with specified minimum benefits. Mental illnesses that are to be covered at same levels as treatment for physical disease are schizophrenia, paranoia, bipolar disorder, autism, and major depression (Tit. 24-A Sec. 2325-A; 24-A Sec. 2749-C: 24-A Sec. 2843; 24-A Sec. 2849-B).

Metabolic formula and special modified low-protein foods for inborn error of metabolism (Tit. 24-A Sec. 2745-B; 24-A Sec. 2837-D; 24-A 4238; 24-A Sec. 2320-D).

Reconstruction of breast on which mastectomy has been performed, and also reconstruction of both breasts to produce symmetrical appearance (Tit. 24-A Sec. 2731-A; 24-A Sec. 2745-C; 24-A Sec. 2837-C; 24-A Sec. 4237; 24-A Sec. 2320-C).

Treatment of alcohol and drug dependency (Tit. 24-A Sec. 2329; 24-A Sec. 2842).

Medically appropriate and necessary equipment as certified by the treating physician, insulin oral hypoglycemic agents, monitors, test strips, syringes and lancets, and outpatient self-management training and educational services. Educational services must be authorized by the state's Diabetes Control Project (Tit. 24-A Sec. 2332-F; 24-A Sec. 2754; 24-A Sec. 2847-E; 24-A Sec. 4240).

Drugs used to treat cancers of a different type than approved by FDA, if recommended in medical literature (Tit. 24 Sec. 2320-F; 24-A Sec. 2745-E; 24-A Sec. 2837-F; 24-A Sec. 4234-D).

Off-label drugs for AIDS treatment (Tit. 24 Sec. 2320-G; 24-A Sec. 2745-F; 24-A Sec. 2837-G; 24-A Sec. 4234-E).

Home health care (Tit. 24 Sec. 2320; 24-A Sec. 2745).

MARYLAND

Baseline mammograms for women ages 35–39, mammograms every 2 years for women ages 40–49, and mammograms every year for women age 50 and over, without deductibles (Sec. 15-814).

Prostate cancer screening for men between the ages of 40 and 75 (Sec. 15-825).

Treatment of cleft palate and cleft lip (Sec. 15-818).

Well-child care to at least specified minimums (Sec. 15-817).

No exclusion of outpatient benefits for all expenses arising from in vitro fertilization procedures, according to certain conditions (Sec. 15-810).

Treatment of mental illness and emotional disorders, with specified minimum benefits (Sec. 15-802).

Medical foods prescribed by doctor for therapeutic treatment of inherited metabolic disease (Sec. 15-807).

Reconstructive breast surgery resulting from mastectomy, including reconstruction surgery on nondiseased breast to achieve symmetry (Sec. 15-815).

Prosthetic devices and orthopedic braces (Ins. Secs. 15-820; 15-839).

Treatment of substance abuse to specified limits (Sec. 15-802).

Care of Alzheimer's disease, including nursing home care (Sec. 15-801).

Home health care (Sec. 15-808).

Offer of coverage for hospice care (Sec. 15-809).

Equipment, supplies, and self-management training in connection with the treatment of diabetes (Sec. 15-822).

Bone mass measurement for preventive diagnosis and treatment of osteoporosis (Sec. 15-823).

All policies and contracts that cover prescription drugs must cover a 90-day supply of a maintenance drug in a single dispensing of the prescription (Sec. 15-824).

Drugs used for contraception, on the same terms and conditions as all other drugs (Sec. 15-826).

Costs of participating in clinical trials (Sec. 15-827).

Anesthesia and hospitalization for dental procedures for patients under 7, and in other specified circumstances (Sec. 15-828).

Annual chlamydia screening test for both women and men, based on qualifying factors (Sec. 15-829).

No restriction on the use of a community pharmacy in place of a mail-order pharmacy (Sec. 15-805).

No exclusion for procedures involving bones or joints in the face, neck, and head (Sec. 15-821).

No exclusion of a drug on grounds that the drug is being used for other purposes than approved by the FDA, if the drug treatment is recognized in at least one standard reference compendium (Sec. 15-804).

No requirement of prior authorization before calling 911 (Sec. 15-126).

Occupational, physical and speech therapy to age 19, for children with congenital and genetic birth defects (Sec. 15-835).

Hair prostheses for cancer patients (Sec. 15-836).

MASSACHUSETTS

Baseline mammograms for women ages 35–39 and mammograms every year for women age 40 and over (Ch. 175:47G; 176A:8J; 176:4I; 176G:4).

Annual Pap screening (Ch. 175:47G; 176A:8J; 176G:4).

Preventive care services to age 6 (Ch. 175:47C).

Diagnosis and treatment of infertility to the same extent as benefits provided for pregnancy-related procedures. Infertility services are included in preventive services that are required to be provided by HMOs. Coverage is mandatory for all non-experimental infertility procedures and infertility-related drugs. Insurers are given option of covering experimental procedures, surrogacy, and sterilization reversal procedures. Prohibited and permissible limitations on coverage are specified (Ch. 175:47H; 176A:8K; 176B:4J; 176G:4).

Treatment of mental illness, with specified minimum benefits (Ch. 175:47B; 176A:8A; 176B:4A).

Special medical formulas necessary for treatment of PKU, as part of coverage of newborns (Ch. 175:47C; 176A:8B; 176B:4C).

Treatment of alcohol abuse, at least to specified limits (Ch. 176A:10; 176B:4A 1/2).

Blood-glucose monitoring strips for treatment of insulin-dependent diabetes (Ch. 175:47N; 176A:8P; 176B:4P; 174G: 4H).

Early intervention services for neurodevelopmental therapy, including speech and physical therapy, from birth until third birthday (Ch. 175:47C; 176A:8B; 176B:4C; 176G:4).

Cardiac rehabilitation expense (Ch. 175:47D; 176A:8G; 176B:4A).

Off-label use of drugs for cancer treatment (Ch. 175:47K; 176A:8N; 176B:4N).

Drugs used to treat cancers of a different type than approved by FDA, if recommended in medical literature (Ch. 175:47K to 175:47L; 176A:8N; 176B:4N; 176G:4E).

Off-label drugs for AIDS treatment, if recommended in at least one standard research compendium (Ch 175:47O to 175: 47P; 176A:8Q; 176B:4P; 176G:4G).

Bone-marrow transplants for persons diagnosed with breast cancer that has progressed to metastic disease (Ch. 175:47R; 176A:8O; 176B:4O; 176G:4F).

Nonprescription enteral formulas for malabsorption caused by diseases such as Crohn's disease and ulcerative colitis (Ch. 175:47I; 176A:8L; 176B:4K; 176G:4D).

Scalp hair prosthesis for hair loss suffered due to cancer or leukemia treatment if a doctor certifies it is medically necessary, with limit of $350 a year (Ch. 175:47T; 176A:8I; 176B: 4R; 176G:4J).

MICHIGAN

Offer of baseline mammograms for women ages 35–39 and mammograms every year for women age 40 and over (Secs. 333.21054; 500.3406d; 500.3616; 550.416; 550.416A).

Offer of coverage for prosthetic devices to maintain or replace body parts removed during mastectomy surgery. Reasonable charges for medical care and reconstructive surgery must be covered (Secs. 500.3406a; 500.1415; 500.3613).

Offer of coverage for hospice care (Secs. 500.3406c; 500.3615).

Drugs used in antineoplastic therapy and the reasonable cost of administration (Secs. 333.21054b; 500.3406e; 500.3616a; 550.1416a).

Inpatient care for substance abuse, and outpatient or intermediate care to specified limits (Secs. 500.3609a; 500.3425; 550.1414a).

MINNESOTA

Routine cancer screening procedures, such as mammograms and Pap smears, when ordered by physician (Sec. 62A.30).

Treatment of cleft palate (Sec. 62A.042).

Child health supervision services through age 12, exempt from deductibles, co-payments, and dollar limitations (Sec. 62A.047).

Mental illness to at least specified minimum benefits (Sec. 62A.152).

Dietary treatment for PKU (Sec. 62A.26).

Reconstructive surgery following surgery or illness of the involved part (Sec. 62A.25).

Treatment of alcohol and substance abuse (Sec. 62A.149).

Treatment of TMJ and craniomandibular disorder (Sec. 62A.043).

Supplies needed for diabetes treatment at same deductible and coinsurance provisions as medical equipment or prescriptions, and also must cover outpatient self-management training and education, including medical nutrition therapy (Sec. 62A.45).

No special restrictions may be imposed upon treatment for Lyme disease that health plan does not apply to nonpreventive treatment in general (Sec. 62A.265).

Drugs used to treat cancers of a different type than approved by FDA, if recommended in medical literature (Sec. 62A.525).

Elimination of port wine stains, with no increase in rates allowed (Sec. 62A.304).

Treatment of breast cancer by high-dose chemotherapy with autologous bone marrow transplant (Sec. 62A.309).

All contracts must cover scalp hair prosthesis for hair loss suffered because of alopecia areata, subject to co-payment, deductibles, and a $350 annual maximum (Sec. 62A.28).

Coverage for chiropractic services (Sec. 62A.15).

Anesthesia and hospitalization for dental procedures for children under age 5 and in other specified circumstances (Sec. 62A.308).

MISSISSIPPI

Annual mammograms for women age 35 and over (Sec. 83-9-108).

Optional coverage for child immunizations (Sec. 83-9-34).

Treatment of mental illness (Secs. 83-9-39 to 83-9-41).

Treatment of alcohol abuse with same terms and conditions as other benefits (Secs. 83-9-27 to 83-9-31).

Treatment of TMJ and craniomandibular disorder at same level as any other joint in the body (Sec. 83-9-45).

Offer of coverage for equipment and supplies used in connection with diabetes management, including supplies for monitoring blood glucose and insulin self-administration (Sec. 83-9-46).

No exclusion of off-label drugs for the treatment of cancer (Sec. 83-9-8).

No requirement that persons use only mail-order pharmacies instead of community pharmacies (Sec. 83-9-6).

Offer of anesthia and hospitalization for dental procedures for children and mentally handicapped adults in appropriate circumstance (Sec. 83-9-32).

MISSOURI

Baseline mammograms for women ages 35–39, mammograms every 2 years for women ages 40–49, and mammograms every year for women age 50 and over, upon the recommendation of a physician where the patient, her mother, or her sister has a prior history of breast cancer (Sec. 376.782).

Child health supervision services through age 6 (Sec. 376.801).

Immunizations for children (Sec. 376.1215).

Treatment of mental illness to at least specified minimum benefits (Sec. 376.827).

Prosthetic devices or reconstructive surgery necessary to restore symmetry. (Sec. 376.1209).

Treatment for alcoholism, chemical dependency, and drug addiction to at least specified minimums (Sec. 376.779).

Equipment, supplies and self-management training for treatment of diabetes (Sec. 376.385).

Dose-intensive chemotherapy/autologous bone marrow transplants or stem cell transplants for treatment of breast cancer. Contracts may contain provisions imposing a lifetime benefit maximum of not less than $100,000 for the chemotherapy/bone marrow transplant or stem cell transplants (Sec. 376.1200).

Offer of coverage for loss or impairment of speech or hearing to same extent as other covered services (Sec. 376.781).

Dietary formulas for treatment of PKU (Sec. 376.1219).

Anesthesia and hospitalization for dental procedures for person under 5, and in other specified circumstances (Sec. 376.1225).

No requirement of prior authorization for emergency services necessary to screen and stabilitize a patient (Sec. 376.1367).

MONTANA

Baseline mammograms for women ages 35–39, mammograms every 2 years for women ages 40–49 or more frequently if recommended by a physician, and mammograms every year for women age 50 and over. Coinsurance and deductibles shall be no less favorable than for physical illness, with a minimum payment of $70 (Secs. 33-22-132; 33-22-1827).

Well-child coverage through age 2, including well-patient exams (Secs. 33-22-303; 33-22-512; 33-30-1014; 17:48-6i).

Infertility services in outpatient medical services, both medically necessary and preventive. (Sec. 33-31-102).

Treatment of mental illness to at least specified minimum benefits. There may not be a more restrictive annual or yearly benefit maximum on mental benefits than for other illnesses until 9/30/01. This does not apply if the mental illness benefits raise costs at least 1 percent (Secs. 33-22-701 to 33-22-705).

Dietary formulas for treatment of inborn errors of metabolism (Sec. 33-22-131).

Reconstructive surgery resulting from a mastectomy that resulted from breast cancer, including all stages of one reconstructive surgery on the nondiseased breast to establish symmetry. Benefits include the costs of prostheses and, if the plan covers outpatient X rays or radiation therapy, it must include outpatient chemotherapy after surgery for breast cancer (Sec. 33-22-135).

Treatment of alcoholism and drug abuse to at least specified minimums (Sec. 33-22-703).

No requirement of prior authorization before seeking emergency services (Sec. 33-36-205).

NEBRASKA

Baseline mammograms for women ages 35–39, mammograms every 2 years for women ages 40–49, and mammograms every year for women age 50 and over. Coverage shall be no less favorable than for other radiological exams. Mammogram supplier shall meet the standards of the federal Mammography Quality Standards Act of 1992 (Sec. 44-785).

All group policies that are advertised as "comprehensive" must provide at least specified benefits for alcohol abuse (Secs. 44-769 to 44-781).

No exclusion for coverage for mental or nervous disorders (Sec. 44-782).

Childhood immunizations (Sec. 44-784).

NEVADA

Annual Pap smears for women age 18 and older; baseline mammograms for woman 35–40; and annual mammograms for women 40 and older (Secs. 689A.0405; 689B.0374; 695B.1912; 695C.1735).

Enteral formulas that are medically necessary for treatment of inherited metabolic diseases and up to at least $2,500 per year for special food products prescribed by physicians (Secs. 689A.0423; 689B.0353; 695B.1923; and 695C.1723).

Use of certain drugs for treatment of cancer (Sec. 689A.0404).

Contraceptive drugs and devices and hormone replacement therapy in certain circumstances. (Sec. 689A.0415).

Prosthetic devices and reconstructive breast surgery following mastectomy, including surgery on one or both breasts to re-establish symmetry (Secs. 689A.041; 689B.0375; 695B.191; 695C.171).

Treatment of substance abuse to at least specified levels (Secs. 689A.046; 689B.036; 695B.194; 695C.174).

No exclusion for treatment of the temporomandibular joint (Secs. 689A.0465; 689B.0379; 695B.1931; 695C.1755).

Training and education for self-management of diabetes, subject to same coinsurance and deductibles as for other covered conditions (Secs. 689A.0427; 689B.0357; 695B.1927; 695C.1727).

NEW HAMPSHIRE

Baseline mammograms for women ages 35–39, mammograms every 2 years for women ages 40–49, and mammograms every year for women age 50 and over (Sec. 417-D:2).

Treatment of mental illness and emotional disorders to at least specified minimum benefits (Secs. 415:18-a; 417-E:1; 420-B:8-b).

Nonprescription enteral formulas for treatment of inherited metabolic disease (Secs. 415:6-c; 415:18-e; 419:5-f; 420:5-g; 420-A:17; 420-B:8-ff).

Reconstruction of a breast on which a mastectomy has been performed and surgery and reconstruction of the other breast to produce a symmetrical appearance (Sec. 417-D:2-b).

Medically appropriate and necessary outpatient self-management training for diabetes, including medical nutrition therapy (Secs. 415:6-e; 415:18-f; 420-B:8-k; 420-A:17-a).

Autologous bone marrow transplants treatment for breast cancer (Secs. 415:18-c; 420-A:13; 420-B:8-e).

Anesthesia and hospitalization for dental procedures for patients less than four years old, and in other specified circumstances (Secs. 415:18g; 420-A:17-b; 420-B:8-cc).

Off-label prescription drugs (Secs. 415: 6-g; 415:18-j).

Outpatient contraceptive services (Sec. 415:18-i).

Scalp hair prosthesis for hair loss suffered because of alopecia areata, alopecia totalis, or permanent loss due to injury, subject to a written recommendation by a doctor as to medical necessity (Secs. 415:18-d; 420-A:14; 420-B:8-f).

NEW JERSEY

Baseline mammograms for women ages 35–39, mammograms every 2 years for women ages 40–49, and mammograms every year for women age 50 and over. Group plans must cover Pap smears to same extent as for any other medical condition (Secs. 17B:27-46-1f; 17:48-6g; 17:48E-35.4; 17:48E-35.12; 17B:26-2.1e; 17:48A-7f; 26:2J-4.4).

Annual diagnostic exam, including digital rectal exam and a prostate specific antigen test, for men age 50 and over and for men age 40 and over who have a family history or other prostate cancer risk factors (Secs. 17:48E-35.13; 17:48-6p; 17B:27-46.1o; 17:48A-7n; 26:2J-4.13).

Specified health examinations and well-baby care benefits (Secs. 17B:27-46-1h; 17B:26-2.1h; 17:48E-35.6; 7:48-6i; 17:48A-7h).

Treatment of metabolic disease, including purchase of medical foods (Secs. 17:48-6s, 17:48A-7q, 17:48E-35.16; 17B:26-2.1o; 17B:27-46l r; 17B:27A-7.4; 17B:27A-19.6; 26:2J-4.17).

Reconstructive surgery following mastectomy, including surgery to restore and achieve symmetry, and costs of prosthesis, and, if cover outpatient X ray or radiation then also cover cost of chemotherapy in connection with treatment of breast cancer (Secs. 17B:27-46.1a; 17:48-6b; 17B:26-2.1a; 17:48A-7b; 17:48E-35; 26:2J-4.14).

Treatment of alcoholism the same as other illnesses (Secs. 17B:27-46.1; 17:48E-34; 17:48-6a; 17B:26-2.1; 17:48A-7a).

Equipment, supplies, and self-management education for treatment of diabetes (Secs. 17B:26-2.1; 17B:27-46.1m; 17:48-6n; 17:48A-71; 17:48E-35.11; 26:2J-4.11).

Blood products and equipment for at-home treatment of hemophilia, with coverage to same extent as other illnesses (Secs. 17B:27-46.1c; 17B-26-2.1c; 17:48E-35.1, 17:48-6d).

Use of off-label drugs for treatment for which they have not been approved by the FDA if the drug is recognized as being medically appropriate for the specific treatment in a listed reference compendium (Secs. 17:48-6h; 17B:26-2.1g; 17B:27-46.1g; 17:48E-35.5; 17:48A-7g; 26:2J-4.5).

Dose-intensive chemotherapy/autologous bone marrow transplants and peripheral blood stem cell transplants (Secs. 17:48-6k; 17:48A-7j; 17:48E-35-8; 17B:26-2.1j; 17B:27-46.1j; 26:2J-4.8).

Audiology and speech-language pathology when deemed by physician to be medically necessary (Secs. 17B:26-2.1p; 17:48A-7r; 17:48E-35.17; 17B:27-46.1e).

Home health care (Secs. 17B:27-51.4; 17B:26-41).

Treatment for chiropractic services (Sec. 17B:27-51.1).

No requirement that subscribers must use mail-order pharmacies (Secs 17B:27-46.1i; 17:48-6j; 17:48A-7i; 17-48E-35.7; 17B:26-2.1i; 26: 2j-4.7).

Treatment of Wilm's tumor, including autologous bone-marrow transplants, even if they are deemed experimental (Secs. 17:48-6f; 17:48A-7e; 17:48E-35.3; 17B:26-2.1d; 17B:27-46.1e; 26:2J-4.8).

NEW MEXICO

Baseline mammograms for women ages 35–39, mammograms every 2 years for women ages 40–49, and mammograms every year for women age 50 and over (Secs. 59A-22-39; 59A-46-41).

Offer of Pap tests for women age 18 and older (Secs. 59A-22-40; 59A-46-42).

Childhood immunizations and booster doses, as recommended by American Academy of Pediatrics, subject to deductibles and coinsurance (Secs. 59A-22-34.3; 59A-46-38.2).

Offer of coverage for alcohol abuse with at least specified limits (Secs. 59A-23-6; 59A-47-35).

Coverage for TMJ and craniomandibular disorder (Sec. 59A-16-13.1).

Medically appropriate and necessary equipment for diabetes as certified by the treating physician, as well as insulin, oral hypoglycemic agents, monitors, test strips, syringes, injection aids, lancets, and outpatient self-management training and educational services, subject to coinsurance and deductibles consistent with other benefits (Secs. 59A-22-41; 59A-46-43).

Offer of coverage for home health care (Secs. 59A-22-36; 59A-46-40; 59A-46-27).

NEW YORK

Baseline mammograms ages 35–39, every 2 years ages 40–49, every year age 50 and over or at any age for high-risk persons (Secs. 3216(i)(11); 3221(1)(11)).

Pap smears for women over the age of 18 (Secs. 3216(i)(15); 3221(1)(14)).

Preventive and primary care services to age 19, not subject to deductibles and coinsurance (Secs. 3216(i)(17); 3221(1)(8)).

Diagnosis and treatment of correctable medical conditions resulting in infertility (Secs. 3216(i)(13); 3221(k)(6)).

Coverage for mental, nervous, or emotional distress to levels specified (Sec. 3221(1)(5)).

Equipment, supplies, and self-management training and education for the treatment of diabetes (Secs. 3216(i)(16); 3221(h)(7)).

Cost of enteral formulas when prescribed as medically necessary for disorders that will cause the person to become malnourished. Include modified solid food products that are medically necessary; cost not to exceed $2,500 per 12-month period (Secs. 3216(i)(21); 3221(k)(11)).

Reconstructive breast surgery resulting form mastectomy, including reconstructive surgery on nondiseased breast to achieve symmetry (Secs. 3216(i)(20); 3221(k)(10)).

Diagnosis and treatment of alcoholism and substance abuse, to specified minimum limits (Sec. 3221(1)(6)).

Treatment of chiropractic services (Secs. 3216(i)(21); 3221(k) (11)).

No exclusions for diagnosis and treatment of medical condition solely because condition results in infertility (Secs. 3216(i)(13); 3221(h)(6)).

Home health care (Secs. 3216(i)(16); 3221(k)(1).

Nursing home and hospice care (Secs. 3221(1)(2) and (10)).

Use of off-label drugs for treatment of cancer (Secs. 3216(i) (12); 3221(1)(12)).

Second opinions for diagnosis of cancer (Secs. 3216(i)(19); 3221(k)(9).

No requirement of prior authorization before seeking emergency services (Sec. 4902(8)).

NORTH CAROLINA

Baseline mammograms for women ages 35–39, mammograms every 2 years for women ages 40–49, mammograms every year for women age 50, and mammograms more frequently if recommended by a physician (Secs. 58-51-57; 58-67-76; 58-65-92).

Pap smears once a year, or more frequently if recommended by a physician (Secs. 58-51-57; 58-67-76; 58-65-92).

Prostate-specific antigen (PSA) tests, with same deductibles and coinsurance as other procedures (Secs. 58-51-58; 58-67-77; 58-65-93).

Treatment of cleft palate and cleft lip (Sec. 58-51-30).

No exclusion for treatment of TMJ caused by deformity, disease, or accident. A contract paying for any procedures involving bones or joints may not exclude coverage for same procedures involving bones and joints of face (Sec. 58-3-121).

Diabetes self-management training, supplies and equipment, and laboratory procedures (Secs. 58-51-61; 58-65-91; 58-67-74).

Drugs used to treat cancers of a different type than approved by FDA if recommended in medical literature (Secs. 58-51-59; 58-65-94; 58-67-78; 58-50-156).

Reconstructive surgery following mastectomy, including surgery on nondiseased breast to achieve symmetry performed at the same time, as well as prostheses and physical complications (Secs. 58-51-62; 58-65-96; 58-67-79).

Treatment of alcohol or drug dependency to at least specified minimums (Secs. 58-51-50; 58-65-75; 58-67-70).

NORTH DAKOTA

Baseline mammograms for women ages 35–39, mammograms every 2 years or more frequently if ordered by doctor for women ages 40–49, and mammograms every year for women age 50 and over (Sec. 26.1-36-09.1).

Annual digital rectal exam and prostate-specific antigen (PSA) test for men 50 and over, African-American men 40 and over, and all men 40 and over if family history of prostate cancer (Sec. 26.1-36-09.6).

Preventive health care to age 5. (Sec. 26.1-36-09.4).

Treatment of mental illness with at least specified minimum benefits (Sec. 26.1-36-09).

Medical foods and low-protein modified food products for therapeutic treatment of inherited metabolic disease (Sec. 26.1-36-09.7).

Treatment of TMJ and craniomandibular disorder, with a $10,000 maximum for surgery and a $2,500 maximum for non-surgical treatment (Sec. 26.1-36-09.3).

Use of drugs for treatment for which they have not been approved by the FDA if the drug is recognized as being medically appropriate for the specific treatment in a listed reference compendium (Sec. 26.1-36-06.1).

Treatment of alcoholism, drug addiction, and other related illnesses, at least to specified minimums (Sec. 26.1-36-08).

No restriction on choice of pharmacy by subscribers (Sec. 26.1-36-12.2).

Offer of coverage for chiropractors (Sec. 26.1-36-06).

Anesthesia and hospitalization for dental procedures for children under 9 and in other circumstances (Sec. 26.1-36-09.0).

OHIO

Offer of baseline mammograms for women ages 35–39, mammograms every 2 years (or more frequently if ordered by doctor) for women ages 40–49, and mammograms every year for women age 50 and over, not to exceed $85 per year or lower amount in contract. Pap smears shall also be mandatory (Secs. 3923.52 to 3923.54; 1751.62).

Health supervision services to age 9, subject to reasonable co-insurance and deductibles. Benefits are limited to $500 during first year of child's life and $150 each year thereafter (Secs. 3923.55 to 3923.56).

Use of drugs to treat cancers of a different type than approved by FDA if recommended in medical literature (Secs. 3923.60 to 3923.61; 1751.66).

No requirement of prior authorization before seeking emergency services (Sec. 3923.65).

Baseline mammograms for women ages 35–39, mammograms every 2 years for women ages 40–49, and mammograms every year for women age 50 and over (Sec. 6060).

Annual prostate screening in men over 40 in high risk categories, and for all men over 50 (Sec. 6060.8).

Child immunization services for children up to age 18 (Sec. 6060.4).

Health supervision services through age 18 (Sec. 3203).

Reconstruction and prosthesis following a mastectomy (Sec. 6060.5).

Treatment of severe mental illness with same coverage provided for other illness and disease, meaning same duration of coverage, limits, deductibles, and coinsurance. Contracts must include coverage for schizophrenia, bipolar disorder, and major depression. A health plan that experiences a greater than 2 percent increase in costs pursuant to providing this coverage is exempt from the requirement (Sec. 6060.11).

Equipment, supplies, and self-management education and training to treat diabetes (Sec. 6060.2).

Bone density tests for qualified individuals (Sec. 6060.1).

Audiological services and hearing aids for children up to the age of 13 (Sec. 6060.7).

Use of drugs to treat cancers of a different type than approved by FDA if recommended in medical literature (Sec. 1-2604).

Anesthesia and hospitalization for dental procedures for children 8 and under, and in other specified circumstances (Sec. 6060.6).

OREGON

Baseline mammograms for women over 40, or as recommended by a physician (Sec. 743.727).

Annual Pap smears for women ages 18–64, or at any time upon referral of provider (Sec. 743.728).

Treatment of mental illness with at least specified minimum benefits. The coverage may be subject to the same provisions as other types of health coverage, and must have the same deductible and coinsurance as for other illness (Sec. 743.556).

Nonprescription enteral formulas for inborn errors of metabolism, including diagnosis, monitoring and controlling disorders, and medical foods (Sec. 743.726).

Self-management education program for treatment of diabetes (Sec. 743.704).

Use of drugs for treatment for which they have not been approved by the FDA if the drug is recognized as being medically appropriate for the specific treatment in a listed reference compendium (Secs. 743.695 to 743.697).

Maxillofacial prosthetic devices (Sec. 743.706).

Treatment of alcohol abuse (Secs. 743.412; 743.556).

PENNSYLVANIA

Annual gynecological exams, including pelvic exam and clinical breast exam. Baseline mammograms for women under 40 and annual mammograms after age 50 (Sec. 764c).

Routine Pap smears (Sec. 1572).

Child immunizations, with coinsurance provisions but exempt from deductibles (Secs. 772, 3503).

Treatment of serious mental illness to at least specified minimums (Sec. 764g).

Education, supplies, and self-management education and training for control of diabetes (Sec. 764e).

Prosthetic devices and reconstructive surgery incident to the mastectomy, subject to usual coinsurance and deductibles. Coverage may be limited to surgical procedures performed within six years of the mastectomy. (Sec. 764d).

Alcohol abuse and other drug abuse and dependency to at least specified levels (Sec. 908-2).

Hearing aids (Sec. 764f).

RHODE ISLAND

Mammograms in accordance with American Cancer Society Guidelines. Payment need be made only if the facility meets quality assurance standards (Secs. 42-62-26; 27-20-17; 27-19-20; 27-41-30; 27-18-41).

Pap smears in accordance with American Cancer Society Guidelines (Secs. 42-62-26; 27-20-17; 27-19-20; 27-41-30; 27-18-41).

Pediatric preventive care to age 19 (Sec. 27-38.1-2).

Diagnosis and treatment of infertility treatment the same as for other pregnancy-related procedures (Secs. 27-18-30; 27-41-33; 27-19-23; 27-20-20).

Treatment of mental illness the same as other illness and disease. Coverage must include same duration of coverage, limits, deductibles, and coinsurance. Coverage includes schizophrenia, bipolar disorder, and major depression (Sec. 27-38.2-2).

Equipment and supplies to treat insulin-treated diabetes, noninsulin-treated diabetes, and gestational diabetes. Coverage includes medically necessary visits to medical nutrition therapists (Secs. 27-18-38; 27-19-35; 27-20-30; 27-41-44).

Use of drugs to treat cancers of a different type than approved by FDA if recommended in medical literature (Secs. 27-55-1 to 27-55-3).

Prosthetic devices and reconstructive surgery to restore symmetry after mastectomy, if performed within 18 months (Secs. 27-18-39; 27-19-34; 27-20-29; 27-41-43).

New cancer therapies still under investigation if they meet certain guidelines (Secs. 27-18-36; 27-19-32; 27-20-27; 27-41-41).

Human leukocyte antigen tests (Secs. 27-18-49; 27-19-41; 27-20-36; 27-41-50).

SOUTH CAROLINA

Baseline mammograms for women ages 35–40, mammograms every 2 years for women ages 40–50, and mammograms every year for women age 50 and over (Sec. 38-71-145).

Pap smears will be covered annually, or more often at doctor's recommendation (Sec. 38-71-145).

Prostate cancer screenings in accordance with guidelines of American Cancer Society (Sec. 38-71-145).

Treatment of cleft palate and cleft lip (Sec. 38-71-240).

Prosthetic devices and reconstructive surgery to restore symmetry after mastectomy (Sec. 38-71-130).

Offer of rider for psychiatric benefits with minimum of $2,000 coverage per member per benefit year. Coverage must include mental and nervous conditions and other psychiatric disorders described in referenced material (Sec. 38-71-737).

Use of drugs to treat cancers of a different type than approved by FDA if recommended in medical literature (Sec. 38-71-275).

SOUTH DAKOTA

Baseline mammograms for women ages 35–39, mammograms every 2 years for women ages 40–49, and mammograms every year for women age 50 and over (Secs. 58-18-36; 58-41-35.5; 58-40-20, 58-38-22; 58-17-1.1; 58-17A-4.1).

Treatment and diagnosis of biologically based mental illness, with same dollar limits, deductibles, coinsurance factors, and restrictions as for other illnesses (Secs. 58-17-98; 58-18-80; 58-18B; 58-38; 58-40; 58-41-115).

Testing and treatment of PKU, including dietary management and formulas (Sec. 58-17-62).

Treatment of alcohol abuse (Secs. 58-17-30.5; 58-18-7.1; 58-41-35.1; 58-40-10.1; 58-38-11.1).

No restrictions on the choice of pharmacy by subscribers (Sec. 58-18-37).

TENNESSEE

Baseline mammograms for women ages 35–39, mammograms every 2 years for women ages 40–49, and mammograms every year for women age 50 and over. Contracts must provide baseline mammograms to women 30–40 years of age if they cover mastectomy surgery (Sec. 56-7-2502).

Early detection of prostate cancer for men age 50 and over or earlier if determined necessary by the physician (Sec. 56-7-2354).

Treatment of mental illness to specified minimum benefits (Sec. 56-7-2601).

Formulas necessary for treatment of PKU, the same as prescription drugs (Sec. 56-7-2505).

Off-label uses of approved drugs (Sec. 56-7-2352).

Anesthesia and hospitalization for dental procedures for children 8 years old or less, under specified circumstances (Sec. 56-7-2353).

Reconstructive breast surgery on diseased breast as well as any surgical procedure on non diseased breast to achieve symmetry (Sec. 56-7-2507).

Treatment of alcoholism and drug dependency (Sec. 56-7-2602).

Offer of medically appropriate and necessary equipment for treatment of diabetes as certified by the treating physician, insulin, oral hypoglycemic agents, monitors, test strips, syringes, injection aids, lancets, and outpatients self-management training and educational services, subject to coinsurance and deductibles consistent with other benefits (Sec. 56-7-2605).

Offer of coverage for treatment of speech and hearing disorders (Sec. 56-7-1011).

Use of drugs to treat cancers of a different type than approved by FDA if recommended in medical literature (Sec. 56-7-2352).

Offer of bone mass measurement for the diagnosis and treatment of osteoporosis (Sec. 56-7-2506).

Treatment of cancer by dose-intensive chemotherapy/autologous bone marrow transplant or stem cell transplants (Sec. 56-7-2504).

Offer of chylamydia screening (Sec. 56-7-2606).

No requirement of prior authorization before seeking emergency services if symptoms indicate emergency medical condition could exist (Sec. 56-7-2355).

TEXAS

Annual mammography screenings for women age 35 and over (Sec. 3.70-2(H)).

Annual diagnostic examination for prostate cancer for men age 50 and older, or age 40 and older with family history of prostate cancer (Sec. 21.53F).

Offer of coverage for in vitro fertilization subject to certain conditions (Sec. 3.51.6).

Treatment of serious mental illness with same limits, deductibles and coinsurance factors as physical illness (Sec. 3.51-14).

Formulas necessary for treatment of PKU (Sec. 3.79).

Reconstruction and prosthesis following mastectomy, subject to same deductible and co-pay as mastectomy (Sec. 21.53D).

Treatment of substance abuse (Sec. 3.51-9).

Treatment of TMJ comparable to coverage provided for all skeletal joints (Sec. 21.53A).

Equipment, supplies, and self-management training programs for the treatment of diabetes, subject to deductible and coinsurance no greater than that for other conditions (Sec. 21.53G).

Diagnosis, treatment, and management of osteoporosis (Sec. 21.53C).

No contract may exclude a service from coverage solely because the service was provided through telemedicine rather than face-to-face contact (Sec. 21.53F).

Offer of coverage for loss of speech and hearing (Sec. 3.70-2 (G).

UTAH

Special dietary products for those suffering from hereditary metabolic disease (Sec. 31A-22-623).

Offer of coverage for treatment of alcohol or drug dependency (Sec. 31A-22-715).

Mental health coverage (Secs. 31A-22-625; 31A-22-720).

Dietary products used for treatment of inborn error of amino acid or urea cycle metabolism (Sec. 31A-22-623).

Diabetes (Sec. 31A-22-626).

VERMONT

Annual mammography screening for women age 50 and older and for those younger upon recommendation of provider, subject to same coinsurance and deductible as other radiological exams (Sec. 4100a).

Offer of coverage for mental illness, after payment of a premium, at least equal to specified minimum benefits (Sec. 4089).

Medical foods prescribed for medically necessary treatment for an inherited metabolic disease. Coverage for low-protein modified food products must be at least $2,500 per 12-month period (Tit. 8 Sec. 4089e).

Treatment of alcohol abuse, to at least specified levels (Secs. 4097 to 4100; 4089b).

Diagnosis and treatment for a musculoskeletal disorder that affects any bone or joint in the face, neck, or head (Sec. 4089g).

Medically necessary growth-cell-stimulating-factor injections taken as part of a prescribed chemotherapy regimen (Sec. 8079e).

Equipment, supplies, and self-management training and education for the treatment of diabetes (Sec. 4089c).

VIRGINIA

Baseline mammograms for women ages 35–39, mammograms every 2 years for women ages 40–49, and mammograms every year for women age 50 and over, with a $50 limit of coverage. These contracts also will provide coverage for annual Pap smears (Sec. 38.2-3418.1).

Pap smears (Sec. 38.2-3418.1:2).

Annual examinations for prostate cancer for men age 50 and over or age 40 and over for high risk persons (Sec. 38.2-3418.7).

Health supervision coverage through age 6, not subject to co-insurance and deductibles. Well-child care is a part of basic health care services required to be provided by HMOs (Sec. 38.2-3411.1).

Treatment of mental illness the same as other illnesses except may be limited to 30 days per policy year (Sec. 38.2-3412.1).

Reconstructive breast surgery (Sec. 38.2-3418.4).

Treatment of substance abuse no more restrictively than for other illness (Sec. 38.2-3412.1).

Equipment, supplies, and self-management training and education for the treatment of diabetes (Sec. 38.2-3418.10).

Treatment of TMJ comparable to coverage provided for all skeletal joints (Sec. 38.2-3418.2).

Hemophilia and congenital bleeding disorders (Sec. 38.2-3418.3).

Medically necessary early intervention services, including speech therapy and physical therapy from birth to age 3, with a $5,000 benefit per year, subject to the same deductibles and coinsurance as for physical illness (Sec. 38.2-3418.5).

No contract may exclude coverage on the grounds that a drug is being used for other purposes than approved by the FDA if the drug treatment is recognized in at least one standard reference compendium (Sec. 38.2-3407.5).

No exclusion for coverage for prescription drugs (Sec. 38.2-3407.5:1).

Treatment of breast cancer by dose-intensive chemotherapy/autologous bone marrow transplants and peripheral blood stem-cell transplants (Sec. 38.2-3418.1:1).

Colorectal cancer screening (Sec. 38.2-3418.7:1).

Clinical trials for treatment studies on cancer (Sec. 38.2-3418.8).

Hospice care (Sec. 38.2-3418.11).

Hospitalization and anesthesia for dental procedures (Sec. 38.2-3418.12).

Morbid obesity (Sec. 38.2-3418.13).

WASHINGTON

Screening or diagnostic mammography services upon recommendation of physician (Secs. 48.21.225; 48.46.275; 48.44.325; 48.20.393).

Offer of coverage for treatment of mental illness with at least specified minimum (Sec. 48.21.240; 48.44.340; 48.46.290).

Formulas for treatment of PKU (Secs. 48.21.300; 48.65.510; 48.440; 48.20.520).

Reconstructive breast surgery resulting from mastectomy, including breast reduction of nondiseased breast to make it equal in size after reconstructive surgery on diseased breast is performed (Secs. 48.20.330; 48.20.395; 48.21.230).

Treatment of chemical dependency (Secs. 48.21.180; 48.46.350; 48.44.240).

Appropriate and medically necessary equipment and supplies for diabetes, as prescribed. All plans or contracts shall provide outpatient self-management training and education, including medical nutrition therapy (Secs. 48.20.391; 48.21.143; 48.44.315; 48.46.272).

Treatment of TMJ (Secs. 48.21.320; 48.44.460; 48.46.530).

Neurodevelopmental therapy for individuals age 6 and under (Secs. 48.21.310; 48.44.450; 48.46.520).

WEST VIRGINIA

Baseline mammograms for women ages 35–39, mammograms every 2 years for women ages 40–49, and mammograms every year for women age 50 and over (Secs. 33-15-4c; 33-16-3g).

Annual Pap smears (Secs. 33-15-4c; 33-16-3g).

Child immunizations (Secs. 33-15-17; 33-16-12; 33-25A-8c).

Infertility services (Sec. 33-25A-2).

Treatment of alcohol abuse (Sec. 33-16-3c).

No exclusion for breast reconstruction or prosthesis following mastectomy (Sec. 33-42-4).

Offer of coverage for treatment of temporomandibular disorders and craniomandibular disorders, but may permit coverage to be declined by written waiver (Sec. 33-16-3f).

Equipment and supplies for treatment and/or management of diabetes, including blood glucose monitors and other supplies, as well as education for self-management of diabetes (Secs. 33-15C-1; 33-16-16).

Rehabilitation services, unless this option is rejected (Secs. 33-15-4d; 33-16-3h).

Home health care (Sec. 33-16-3b; 33-28-5a).

No exclusion for reconstruction or cosmetic surgery required by injury caused by act of family violence (Sec. 33-42-4).

Colorectal cancer tests (Sec. 33-15-4f).

WISCONSIN

Two mammogram exams between ages 40–49, and annually for women age 50 and older (Sec. 632.895(8)).

Treatment of mental and nervous disorders with at least specified minimum benefits (Sec. 632.89).

Breast reconstruction of the affected tissue, following mastectomy (Sec. 632.895(13)).

Treatment of alcoholism and other drug abuse problems to at least specified minimums (Sec. 632.89).

Treatment of TMJ disorders (Sec. 632.895(11)).

Inpatient and outpatient treatment of kidney disease, at least to specified minimums (Sec. 632.895(4)).

Equipment, supplies, and self-management education and training for treatment of diabetes (Sec. 632.895(6)).

Anesthesia and hospitalization for dental procedures for children under 5 and in other specified circumstances (Sec. 632.895(12)).

Home health care (Sec. 632.895(2)).

Coverage for grandchildren until the children who are the parents of the grandchildren reach the age of 18 (Sec. 632.895(5m)).

WYOMING

"Comprehensive Adult Wellness benefits," not subject to deductibles, that shall provide for exams for breast cancer (Sec. 26-19-107).

"Comprehensive Adult Wellness benefits," not subject to deductibles, that shall provide for exams for cervical cancer (Sec. 26-19-107).

"Comprehensive Adult Wellness benefits," not subject to deductibles, that shall provide for exams for prostate cancer. (Sec. 26-19-107).

"Comprehensive Adult Wellness benefits," not subject to deductibles, that shall provide for exams for diabetes (Sec. 26-19-107).

Taking an Appeal from A to Z: Meaning, from Coverage Denied to Coverage Granted

Like death and taxes, everyone has to deal with improper denials of coverage once in a while. The older you are, and the more children you have, the more likely it is you've had this problem already. But even if you're young and single, you're not exempt from the problem.

Improper denials of coverage are a fact of life in managed care. On the one hand, they are inevitable due to the massive numbers of health claims that are reviewed every day. Bureaucracies make mistakes, which means managed care organizations sometimes deny claims in error.

On the other hand, it is no secret that managed care organizations make money when they don't provide care. Some people believe that managed care organizations deliberately deny a certain percentage of legitimate claims, in hopes that the claimants won't complain and the company will save the money.

Unfortunately the gamble often is a safe one. Most people

don't challenge wrongful coverage denials—especially when the amount of money at stake is small. They figure it isn't worth spending hours on the phone to track down a missing $25 or $30. To many people, it also isn't worth writing appeals letters, attending grievance hearings, and fighting the red tape.

Such apathy can be a mistake. It's a good idea to get into the habit of correcting even the little problems. You will be prepared to handle a major problem, if one ever arises, if you've already tackled a few minor ones. You will also be more effective in resolving your problems if you understand, and don't fear, the grievance process.

Whenever you take on a health insurer or HMO, you'll probably go through basically the same steps. Here are the most common ones:

1. CALL CUSTOMER SERVICE

As soon as you discover that a denial seems wrong, the first step is to call customer service. The customer service department exists, in part, to straighten out errors and keep people like you happy. So call them, and give them a chance to do their jobs.

Before you call, figure out the best way of explaining why you think the denial is wrong. It can be very difficult to explain these things, especially because of all the codes and lingo in managed care. Decide what points you need to make, and which documents prove each of these points. Then write it all down in your annual notebook.

This preparation is good for two reasons. First, it will help to streamline your conversations with customer service and avoid unnecessary ramblings. Second, it will help you to remember what you said and why. Even if you have to start from scratch with customer service in a few months, at least you won't have to figure it all out again.

When you call, try to follow all of the steps set forth in Step Six. In brief, make sure you have your annual insurance folder with you, including your annual notebook; get a cup of coffee and some reading material before you call; try to get your conversations entered into the managed care organization's computer; take notes on all conversations; and find out as much as you can about the people who talk to you. And don't forget to send a letter to the insurance company after every conversation, memorializing the conversation in writing.

Customer service often works. I have resolved many problems, particularly small ones, without going past the customer service department. It can be an infuriating process—you may have to call and write repeatedly for several months, and speak to many different people, before anything happens. But if your problem is not a crisis and you can handle the frustration, it may be worth the wait.

Be very alert when dealing with customer service, though, and pay careful attention to whether you seem to have any hope of resolving your problem at this level. If it seems unlikely that you'll make any progress, move straight to filing a written grievance. In that case you're probably heading there anyhow, so don't waste your time.

When dealing with customer service, try to get one person to assume responsibility for correcting your problem. During your first conversation, find out as much as possible about the person who's trying to help you. Confirm, at the end of the conversation, what actions that person plans to take. Then advise that person that you will call him or her back in two weeks for a status report. Mark your calender, so that you don't forget.

When you call back, try to speak to the same person. Ask to be transferred to that person, if you don't have a direct extension. If you get voice mail, though, it may not be worthwhile to leave a message. It's unlikely that you'll ever get a call back, and you certainly shouldn't count on receiving one.

If you do reach the same person, remind him or her of the earlier conversation and the promise to follow up. There are responsible people in some customer service departments; maybe you'll find out that the representative actually has been working on your problem.

If you can't reach the same person, though, just start again with whoever answered the phone. You won't have a choice and at least you'll have your records to keep you moving forward.

2. CALL YOUR EMPLOYER

If you are insured through an employer, you should try contacting your employer for help once you realize that you definitely have a problem. Lots of employers are cautiously cooperative; I've seen many get good results.

When you speak to your employer, remember that the people you're speaking to: (1) may be responsible for selecting the insurer that you're mad at; and (2) may be responsible for negotiating the next year's premium—which may go up, by the way, if you get the coverage that you want. That means this is not the time for a venting session. In fact, if you indulge in one, it could be viewed as a personal attack upon the people that you're asking for help. So don't do it. Instead, be as matter-of-fact and unemotional as possible about the situation. Just explain the coverage you seek, your basis for the claim, the denial you've received, and the reasons for reversal.

Instead of just handing your problem over to your employer, it's a good idea to work with them. Ask them, for example, for information about the mandatory-benefit laws in your state. Don't let them tell you that the mandatory-benefit laws don't apply to any employer-sponsored health plans owing to ERISA— the U.S. Supreme Court has stated the opposite in a 1985 decision called *Metropolitan Life Insurance Company v. Massachusetts*. In particular, the Supreme Court stated that the state mandatory-benefit laws apply to all employer-sponsored health plans except for the minority that are fully self-funded.

Similarly, ask your employer whether you have a copy of the company's entire health plan. Typically, employees are only given a short version of the health plan, called a Summary Plan Description or SPD. Employers usually keep the actual contract in the human resources department, or the equivalent thereof. Ask to copy, or at least to see, your employer's copy of the contract, and then compare it meticulously to the SPD that you were given.

The comparison is important because sometimes, in trying to write the simplified SPD, the authors incorrectly describe the coverage that actually is provided in the formal contract. But insurers usually continue to follow the formal contract, and deny coverage based on its narrow terms. That may be why you are confused about a coverage denial in the first place—it may match the formal contract, but not the coverage described in your SPD.

Sometimes courts hold that the terms of the SPD are more important than the formal contract, since the SPD is the document that actually is given to employees. Insurance companies know this. So if you do discover that the SPD provides coverage than is not provided by the formal contract, tell your insurance company immediately. Tell them also that you know all about the legal principles that favor the SPD. They may, after some hemming and hawing, quietly reverse the denial.

3. FILE AN INTERNAL GRIEVANCE

If these alternatives don't work, your next step may be to file a grievance. HMOs or managed care plans typically maintain an internal system for handling grievances. "Internal," in this context, means a procedure for the plan itself to reconsider its denials.

Most of these systems require: (1) explicit time periods in which HMOs or managed care plans must respond to complaints and appeals; (2) an expedited appeal process for urgent cases; (3) several levels of review, including consideration by medical specialists when appropriate; and (4) written notice of appeal denials, including the right to pursue appeals further.

In some states, grievances can be oral or written. As a rule, though, it is much safer to file your grievances in writing. Otherwise it may be very hard to prove exactly when you complained and what you said.

There are a few tricks for the best way to handle internal grievances. First, check your policy or plan for a description of the grievance procedure and follow it exactly. For example, send your grievance letter to the address that is required by the plan for grievances. If no address is specified, call customer service and find out where the letter should go.

It is mandatory in most states for managed care plans and health insurers to set forth their grievance procedures in their policies and plans. If you don't find any grievance procedures on a first review, keep looking. They're probably in there somewhere.

Second, send your letter in the exact manner specified in the plan's grievance procedure. If the plan states that grievance letters should be sent by certified mail, return receipt requested, do it. If the plan does not state how the letters should be sent, then it's a good idea to send these letters by an overnight service like express mail or Federal Express. I prefer these services to certified mail for one simple reason. It's very easy for the little green confirmation cards from certified mail to get lost in the mail and, if they do, you may have a real problem. You are less likely to have a problem with an overnight service that has a tracking system.

If you choose an express mail service, remember that you will need a street address, not just a post office box number. These services usually will not deliver mail to post office boxes.

So my third trick is to remember to ask customer service for a street address, and use it if you can get it.

My fourth trick requires a change in your thinking. When you write this letter, you should try to think like a lawyer. That means explaining, persuasively, all of the reasons why the coverage denial was wrong. It also means attaching copies of all the documents that you think prove your claim.

Reread your draft letter critically and repeatedly, and keep it as short as possible. Ask yourself whether *you* would be convinced by these arguments if you worked for the insurance company. Similarly, reread all of the documents that you are attaching. See if any of them hurt your arguments—your insurer would love the chance to use your documents against you. While you're at it, see if the documents really support what you're saying. They won't be helpful if no one but you understands what they say.

Remember that your grievance letter will be read by people who know nothing about the denial you're protesting, your fears and concerns about your health, or the frustrations you've endured with the insurance company. Frankly, they won't care. All they'll care about is whether or not the denial was proper, based on an analysis of your medical records and their internal policies and procedures.

So do *not* treat this letter as a venting session. That will discredit you and make it too easy for this committee to write you off as a nut. Treat this letter like a legal brief—and represent yourself wisely.

Some plans have the practice of responding to your letter by offering you the option of an oral hearing. Think very carefully before you accept. If your case has true sympathy value and you will make an appealing advocate, an oral hearing might be best. But if your case is very complicated and you have nasty, surly feelings toward your HMO, you may be smart to stay away.

Jason Wolff Was Neither Big nor Bad; Still, He Huffed and He Puffed Until He Blew That Denial Away

It all started for Jason Wolff when he went skiing on January 25, 1990. He took a fall while traveling about fifty miles an hour, and his skis hit him in the head. He sliced open his tongue, lips and gums, and lost his two front teeth.

His sister, skiing with him, found the teeth in the snow, and rushed Jason to a nearby hospital. Within a few days, Jason was treated by a battery of doctors, oral surgeons, and endodontists, who cleaned his wounds and reimplanted the front teeth. His health insurer—not his dental insurer—paid.

Five years passed. Then Jason suddenly experienced acute pain in his head and face. He started in again with doctors, dentists, and oral surgeons, and they soon discovered that an infection was eating away at the roots of his teeth and the adjacent bones.

Jason was in extreme pain, and needed surgery as soon as possible. But this time, his health insurer decided that the problem was dental, rather than medical, and that it was not covered.

Jason was lucky. He was able to pay for his medical care on his own, which relieved his physical problems and pain. In the end, he says he had at least fifty appointments with doctors, surgeons, and dentists. He had five different surgeries and his medical bills totalled approximately $13,000.

But Jason also was very determined not to give up on insurance. Throughout these months, he relentlessly pursued his right to reimbursement.

The main problem was that Jason's insurance policy contained two provisions that appeared contradictory. On the one hand, the policy covered "oral surgery services" for conditions that were the result of "congenital defect or accidental injury." On the other hand, the policy stated that "all dental services, including orthodontics, are excluded."

(continued)

Jason hung his hat on the former provision; the insurance company hung its hat upon the latter.

From the end of 1995 until the end of 1996, Jason and his insurance company exchanged letters with regularity. The insurer offered reasons for the denial. Jason knocked them down. The insurer offered new and different reasons. He knocked them down, too. The insurer wrote incomprehensible letters. Jason called the authors and demanded clarifications. He moved from one grievance level to another. He perservered.

Finally the time came for Jason to appear in person at an informal hearing. He prepared carefully and presented his case as well as he could—without spending the time or money to bring in lawyers, doctors, or expert witnesses. In his view, the hearing rapidly deteriorated into a back-and-forth about what the facts were, what the doctors said, what the policy permitted, what the company policies (which Jason had never seen) provided, and so on.

At the end, Jason launched into what he calls his "little soapbox." He delivered an emotional speech about his struggle to obtain coverage, the inequities that he perceived, his inability to obtain a lawyer owing to the ERISA limitations on recovery of damages and, finally, how his physical infirmities were aggravated by what he believed was the insurer's callous treatment of his claim. Then he walked out, certain that he had lost but comforted by having "fought the good fight" and having had his say.

Fifteen days later, Jason received a letter from his insurance company reversing the denial.

Jason was so empowered by the experience that he wrote it all down—on a Web site, for all to see. That's where I first found him (http://members.aol.com/jasonwolff/hmohelp.htm). He even wrote up an "Informal Guide To Appealing Health Insurance Claims," which sets forth some of the basic principles that you've read about here in *Making Them Pay*.

It all worked out for Jason, although he never thought it would. The great news is that it can work out for you, too. Just take a page from Jason's book, and make it happen.

The fifth trick involves taking charge of the information exchange. Typically, insurers do not reveal what information will cause them to reverse the denial. They will simply invite appellants to provide any information that they want the insurers to see. All too often, people are at a loss and end up volunteering nothing; instead, they just answer any questions the insurers choose to ask. This is not a good tactic because the insurers' questions are not designed to produce a reversal of the denial.

The better approach is to think creatively about how to prove your case, and to provide as much helpful information as possible. You should also volunteer information, if there is any, that shows why the denial was an error.

I once represented a surgeon who had lost most of the sight in one eye in a freak accident. This meant that he could not operate anymore, and could only perform relatively minor medical procedures. He applied to his disability insurer for disability coverage, but was turned down. He filed a grievance and was told to submit anything he wanted the insurer to see. He couldn't think of anything except for what the insurer requested: financial information that showed he still was making money (and that didn't show that his postaccident income resulted from late payments for services he had performed before the accident).

It only took one letter to get a complete reversal. The solution lay in finding records that proved his medical practice was basically destroyed by the accident. These records included: (1) a certificate showing that the doctor had dropped his medical malpractice insurance; (2) letters he wrote to hospitals, advising them he could no longer handle emergency cases; and (3) letters he wrote to other doctors, telling them not to refer any more patients to him. He had all of this information in his files all along, but never knew to send it to his disability insurer.

My sixth trick is very important. You should set forth in your letter *all* of the information that supports your position in any way. Because of certain rules and regulations, you may be barred in the future from raising anything that you do not include right now. That goes for arguments you might make as well as documents that you might attach. So think carefully about the entire issue and about all the arguments that help you. This letter may be your one real chance to make your case.

Finally, the seventh trick is to state in this letter that, by filing this grievance, you are not waiving any rights against the insurance company, including your right to file an action in a court of law and seek all appropriate damages, including punitive damages. By making this statement, you may keep the insurance company from trying to use your grievance letter against you.

Including this sentence will not guarantee that you will be free to sue your insurer in a court of law. Other obstacles, like arbitration provisions in your insurance policy, may stand in your way. But there's no harm in putting this reservation-of-rights sentence in your grievance letter. It takes very little effort, and it's well worth your time.

4. FILE AN EXTERNAL GRIEVANCE

If your internal grievance fails, the next step in many cases may be to file an external grievance. External grievances are supposed to be grievances that are reviewed by third parties, and provide a completely independent perspective. Many states have passed laws requiring health plans to participate in such external reviews.

The level of detail in these laws vary widely. Some of them just refer, in broad language, to external review procedures. Others set specific requirements for the review process, the types of appeals eligible for review, and the process for appointing the "independent" reviewers. For example, in some states, the regulatory agency either does the review or selects the reviewers. In other states, the reviewers are selected by either the health plan, the patient, or an independent review organization, known as an IRO, which is appointed by or under contract with the state.

Generally, it works to approach these external procedures in the same fashion as the internal ones, from following the grievance procedure exactly to including the reservation-of-rights sentence. Just reread the section above when you reach this point in the process.

The Kaiser Family Foundation released a detailed study of the external grievance procedures in effect as of November of 1998, called "External Review of Health Plan Decisions: An Overview of Key Program Features in the State and Medicare." The study determined that external grievance procedures are often regarded as effective and fair, especially since they overturn health plan decisions about as frequently as they uphold them. The study also found that no state favored patients more than 60 percent, or less than 30 percent, of the time.

Nevertheless, the study found that people rarely take advantage of external review procedures. According to the study, only forty-nine external reviews were sought in Michigan from 1995 to June 1998. Similarly, in Missouri only sixty external reviews were sought from 1994 though June 1998. The study speculated that there are many possible explanations, but one of them certainly is that many people do not know about, or understand the value of, these procedures.

So don't be one of the people in the dark. Any time you have a gripe with an insurance company, you should ask customer service, and beyond, whether the company offers any external review procedures. Who knows? Maybe just asking the question will help get your gripe resolved.

There are two important caveats to external reviews. First, insurers sometimes try to look as if they're performing external reviews of grievances when they're not. In the course of pursuing an appeal, your insurer may start sending you letters that refer to "external" grievance procedures. Whenever you see these words it's a good idea to be wary.

For example, it's fairly common to call a review "external" when it actually is performed by employees of the insurer—but different ones than the employees who made the denial decision. It's also common for insurance companies to form a panel of three "independent" reviewers, consisting of two employees of the insurance company and one outside doctor—who is selected, appointed, and paid by the insurance company. I don't care what they call this; I don't call it "external."

Second, it is unclear whether the states even have authority to mandate external review procedures for health plans that are governed by ERISA. For example, a federal court in Texas held in 1998, and a higher court later affirmed, that because federal law applies to ERISA plans, the Texas state law regarding external review does not. As of the publication date, the law in this area was in flux. This particular decision was undergoing intense scrutiny by the judiciary as well as the professional Bar. Courts in other states were struggling with this issue as well.

5. FILE A LAWSUIT IN COURT

There is a vigorous national debate about the standards that should be applied to lawsuits against health plans regulated by ERISA, and especially whether people ever should be allowed to seek punitive damages from these plans. This debate exists because of certain legal restrictions that are set forth in the text of the ERISA statute. As discussed in the Introduction, these restrictions affects the more than 100 million people who obtain their health coverage through their employment—the majority of the insured people in the country.

People whose plans fall outside of ERISA do not have such restrictions and are free to seek punitive damages. They have periodically achieved extraordinary results—and the contrast between the results of ERISA cases and non-ERISA cases is dramatic.

Sometimes You Just Have to Make Them Pay

It would not be right to think of David Goodrich as "lucky."

He wasn't lucky in March of 1995, when he succumbed to a rare form of stomach cancer just three years after the initial diagnosis.

He wasn't lucky in the years preceding his death, when his insurance company refused to pay for his chemotherapy.

And he wasn't exactly lucky years later, when a jury in San Bernardino, California, awarded his widow $116 million in punitive damages in an extensively publicized court decision called *Goodrich v. Aetna Life & Casualty Co., Inc.*

But, in a most limited sense, David Goodrich was lucky. Unlike the vast majority of the people who have health insurance in the first place, he did not get his health insurance from a private employer. That meant that it did not fall under ERISA, which in turn meant that his widow was able to sue his insurance company—and seek punitive damages—when it took actions that she believed were unconscionable and fatal.

If her family's health plan had fallen under ERISA, the principal consequence for its refusal to pay for David's chemotherapy would have been the cost of the chemotherapy—paid posthumously.

And, unfortunately, that is what happens to plenty of people in ERISA plans.

That's basically what happened, for example, to one family in New York. In 1992, a man named Joseph Scalamandre lost his wife to breast cancer after their insurance company refused to pay for high-dose chemotherapy. He sued, even though the plan was governed by ERISA.

Scalamandre prevailed on his claim in federal court in a publicly reported decision. But, due to ERISA's limitations on damages, the court

(continued)

limited Scalamandre's recovery to the cost of the denied treatment (about $165,000), plus interest, costs, and attorneys fees.

The outcome was one notch worse for a family in Kansas. Constance Bossemeyer suffered from cancer and her HMO refused to pay for high-dose chemotherapy. She sued in federal court because her plan fell under ERISA. In her case, however, the federal court announced in a publicly reported decision that it was dismissing her lawsuit for failing to satisfy a particular legal standard under ERISA.

When you stop to think about it, ERISA almost gives health plans a financial incentive for refusing particularly expensive medical treatments. By refusing, the health plans would save, and could invest, the money they had been called upon to spend.

If the patients die, their survivors might not have the financial or emotional wherewithal for litigation about the denials, in which case the health plans could just keep the money. And if they are sued, the worst that could happen—give or take some legal fees and interest—would be paying the patients' estates the original contested amounts.

That would be the same to the health plans as if it paid for the expensive treatments years before. But it's not the same to the patients— and certainly not to their survivors.

So while it would not be right to call David Goodrich lucky, it would be fair to call him a hero. On his behalf, his widow perservered in the lawsuit against his insurance company even after his death. She forced the insurer to give David, although posthumously, his day in court.

And, even if David's widow never collects a dime, she'll always know that, in a way that counts, David truly made them pay.

Most consumer and provider groups strongly advocate opening the doors of the courthouse to patients for many reasons. Their reasons include that there is no accountability without liability, and that health insurers and HMOs will be forced to modify their behavior if they are exposed to the risk of punitive damages.

Most insurance companies, obviously, are strongly opposed.

Among other things, they contend that they will be forced to hike their premiums if they are subjected to an increased risk of litigation and punitive damages. They also contend that such lawsuits will simply pad the wallets of the plaintiffs' lawyers, and will not improve health care.

Even if you are not on an ERISA plan, remember that you will often be required to exhaust your administrative remedies before you file a lawsuit. This means that you will need to pursue all of the grievance procedures offered by your health plan before you sue. To satisfy this requirement, it is particularly important for you to do a thorough investigation of exactly what grievance procedures exist for your plan.

Remember, also, to take a cautious view toward the possibility of receiving a multimillion-dollar punitive damages award. While such awards do happen, and receive extensive publicity when they do, they are rare—and are usually reserved for truly horrific situations. It is very easy to lose perspective on your own problem, and decide that it merits the kind of gratifying punishment offered by such dramatic awards. For your sake, I hope that it does not. I also hope you appreciate that most people with health care complaints do *not* receive enormous sums in punitive damages. Place your bets elsewhere.

6. FILE AN ARBITRATION

With increasing frequency, health plans are starting to slip mandatory-arbitration provisions into their policies. These provisions mean that you are waiving your rights to have a judge and jury decide your case. In the event of a coverage dispute, you will be limited to arbitration before a person, or a group of people, who are not judges. You will not have many of the protections of the court system, often including the right to appeal.

Arbitration has strengths and weaknesses. The principal strength is that it is usually resolved more quickly, and with less expense, than litigation in court. The principal weakness is that you lose the protections of the court system.

At some point, courts may consider whether it is fair for insurers to insert mandatory-arbitration provisions in their standard-form contracts. Until then, the best you can do is understand that some policies have this language, and to try to avoid it if possible. *Not* because arbitration is necessarily a bad thing but more because it doesn't seem fair to have your insurer take away your right to a judge and jury without giving you a choice in the matter.

7. ASK THE GOVERNMENT FOR HELP

In addition to the traditional approaches to resolving coverage disputes, you may wish to consider a few roundabout ones. These include filing complaints with government agencies such as state insurance departments, health departments, and departments that regulate corporations. They also include filing complaints with state-funded consumer organizations.

In every state, managed care plans and health insurers are regulated by one or more state agencies. It's a safe bet that one of them is the state's insurance department. These state insurance departments typically accept, and investigate, complaints from consumers regarding HMOs and health insurers. Some of them, like the New York State Insurance Department, even publish annual reports that set forth the number of complaints filed each year against each insurance company and whether those complaints were upheld, dismissed, or still pending.

When you have a complaint against an HMO or health insurer, it's always a good idea to report it to your state insurance department or other appropriate agency. Many insurance companies seem to hate such reports, probably because they lead to bad statistics. They also seem to hate being second-guessed by government agencies. If you're lucky, the governmental oversight will lead to a change of position.

A list of all fifty state insurance departments is attached as Appendix B.

Another traditional government resource is the attorney general's office. Many state attorneys general have become active in health care concerns. In fact, the attorney general of New York even founded a division devoted solely to managed care. A list of the attorneys general of all fifty states, as of 2000, is attached as Appendix C.

In addition to government agencies, some states maintain quasi-governmental resources for consumers. For example, Florida and Vermont have passed laws that establish independent consumer assistance programs. Florida created a Statewide Managed Care Ombudsman Committee, which functions within the Agency for Health Care. Vermont required the state to contract with a nonprofit organization to serve as an Office of Health Care Ombudsman. Both of these agencies were authorized by statute to review, and assist consumers with, health complaints.

Other states use their consumer advocates to serve comparable functions. In New York, for example, the Public Advocate's Office is extremely active in health care matters, and has issued many studies that analyze defects in the health care system. A contact list that identifies some of the organizations that assist consumers through direct assistance, research, or otherwise, is set forth in Appendix D.

CONCLUSION

You really have no excuse for sleeping on your rights when it comes to your health care. There are many different ways to take on your insurance company, and many different organizations that are ready to help you. All you need to do is get started.

GET YOUR SLINGSHOT AND GATHER YOUR STONES: GOLIATH DOESN'T HAVE A CHANCE

There's an old Bible story about David and Goliath. The gist of it is that a horrible, enormous giant named Goliath came to town to make trouble. Everyone was afraid to take him on because he was so big. But one barefoot shepherd named David stepped forward, armed with nothing but a slingshot and some pebbles.

David's first pebbles missed their mark. But then he aimed carefully and hit Goliath right between the eyes. The impossible happened from this well-placed pebble. The deadly giant fell to the ground; David became king of Israel; and the rest, as they say, is history.

Goliath is not a bad analogy for your health insurer. Huge, enormous, capable of making deadly trouble. And David is not a bad analogy for you, when you take on your health insurer: small, barefoot, helpless, and so on.

Until now, though, the analogy has stopped there. You probably haven't felt much like an average guy who uses a pebble to slay a giant. You may have felt more like the pebble the giant stepped on.

But it's time for that to change. You know it, or you wouldn't have read this book.

You've already started gathering your pebbles. The most important is an attitude change. You now know what David knew a long time ago: that the small can knock down the biggest of the big, as long as they think and act carefully, calmly, and strategically.

Another pebble is old-fashioned knowledge. David knew enough about human anatomy to know where to place that ultimate pebble. You have now learned the anatomy of a health plan. This means that you'll know, when the time comes, how to find the shortfalls in every plan and the weak spots in every denial of coverage.

The next pebble is mastering related insurance issues. You will now be savvy about how much your insurance really costs, what you're supposed to get for the money, and what details will make your life easier when it comes to health care.

You've gathered other critical pebbles as well, like learning to keep good records, learning about the mandatory-benefit laws of each state, and learning how to pursue effective appeals.

You're well on your way. Now you can step forward with confidence when it's time to pick a health plan. You can systematically compare your various options and select the one that's best for you.

And, once that's done, you will continue to stand tall. You will understand what benefits you paid for and how to get them. You will keep orderly, useful records with minimum effort. You will recognize mistakes in both payments and denials, and correct them without wasting a lot of time and energy. And you will do this without getting all worked up and emotional, because you've learned how to treat this as just a big game.

Now, like David, you can have confidence in yourself. You know how to make good, smart, strategic decisions. You know how to do it quickly and quietly. And you know how, and where, to aim.

So go out there and get started. You'll save your money, your time, your sanity, and maybe your life. You may even be doing your part, in a small way, to improve the entire messed-up health insurance system.

And you may even find that while you're at it, it's almost (in a crazy sort of way) fun.

APPENDIXES

Composite Health Plan (HMO, with Point-of-Service Option)

The following is a composite health plan for your general reference while reading Steps One through Three. It uses representative language from a large number of health plans and insurance policies. It is not, however, an exact copy of any particular plan or policy, nor does it include every single section that you might expect to find in one of them.

Section I: How the Plan Works

1. The Primary Care Physician

Each person who enrolls in the plan is required to select a Primary Care Physician (PCP). The PCP selected by you becomes your personal Physician and health care advisor who will maintain a complete record of your medical history and health care needs. Your PCP is responsible for coordinating your care and will become familiar with the overall status of your health.

Your PCP is also your key to obtaining the care you need. Whenever you require health care services, you must first contact your PCP. He or she will provide or arrange for the Covered Services you need. Primary Care, which includes routine office visits for treatment of illness and injury as well as Preventive Care, will be provided by your PCP. If your PCP decides that you need to see a Network Specialist, he or she will arrange for you to obtain Specialty Care. Please remember, Primary and Preventive Care that is not provided by your PCP will not be Covered under the Plan.

Female Members may elect a Network OB/GYN in addition to their PCP. Members may see their selected OB/GYN without a referral from their PCP.

2. Speciality Care

If your PCP cannot provide a specific medical service, he or she will give you a referral to a Network Specialist. As part of the referral process, your PCP will complete a referral form. You will be given the form to take with you to your appointment with the Network Specialist. Once you have obtained the referral, you may visit the Network Specialist and receive the Covered Services you need. You cannot obtain Specialty Care without a referral from your PCP. If you see a Network Specialist without a referral, neither the visit nor the services will be Covered, even though the specialist is a Network Specialist.

PLEASE NOTE Referral visits to a Network Specialist cannot exceed the number of visits authorized by your PCP and are only valid for a period of up to ninety days from date of issue. If further visits are necessary, or the referral expires, you must ask your PCP for another referral. Also, referrals become invalid when your coverage under this Certificate terminates.

3. Precertification

All admissions to health care facilities and certain diagnostic tests and therapeutic procedures must be Precertified by us before you are admitted or receive treatment.

Precertification starts with a call to Our Medical Management Department by your PCP or the Network Specialist involved. One of our Medical Management professionals will examine the case, consult with your Physician, and discuss the clinical findings. If all agree the requested admission, test, or procedure is appropriate, the Precertification is provided. This comprehensive evaluation assures that the treatment you receive is appropriate for your needs and is delivered in the most cost-effective setting.

Your Network Physician is responsible for obtaining any required Precertification and is aware of when Precertification is required. However, if you wish to double-check that your Network Physician has contacted us about your case, please feel free to call Customer Service and inquire.

4. Second Opinions

We reserve the right to require a second opinion for any surgical procedure. At the time of Precertification, you may be advised that a second opinion will be required in order for the services to be Covered. If a second opinion is required, we will refer you to a Network Provider for a second opinion.

In the event that the first and second opinions differ, a third opinion will be required. We will designate a new Network Provider. The third opinion will determine whether or not the surgery is Precertified. There will be no cost to you for either the second or third opinion.

You may also request a second opinion.

5. Diagnostic Testing and Laboratory Services

Covered X rays or diagnostic procedures performed at Network facilities will be provided by us without any required Co-payment. If your PCP recommends laboratory testing, remind him or her to use a Network Provider. Unless you are hospitalized or receiving preadmission testing, Hospitals are not Network Providers for these tests.

6. Health Maintenance Organizations

Health maintenance organizations (HMOs) are health plans that require you to see Plan providers: specific physicians, hospitals, and other providers that contract with us. These providers coordinate your health care services. The care you receive includes preventive care such as routine office visits, physical exams, well-baby care and immunizations, as well as treatment for illness and injury.

When you receive services from our providers, you will not have to submit claim forms or pay bills. However, you must pay Co-payments and coinsurance listed in this brochure. When you receive emergency services you may have to submit claim forms.

You should join an HMO because you prefer the plan's benefits, not because a particular provider is available. You cannot change plans because a provider leaves our Plan. We cannot guarantee that any one physician or group of physicians, hospital, or other provider will be available and/or remain under contract with us. Our providers follow generally accepted medical practice when prescribing any course of treatment.

Section II: How to Join the Plan

(This section typically discusses eligibility requirements, such as geographic location, employment status, application procedures, and family structure. This information is beyond the scope of Making Them Pay, *so these sections are not included here.)*

Section III: Facts About the Plan

1. Role of Your Primary Care Doctor

The first and most important decision each Member must make is the selection of a Primary Care Doctor. The decision is important since it is through this doctor that all other health services, particularly those of specialists, are obtained. It is the responsibility of your Primary Care Doctor to obtain any necessary authorizations from the Plan before referring you to a specialist or making arrangements for hospitalization. Services of other providers are covered only when you have been referred by your Primary Care

Doctor, with the following exceptions: a woman may see her Plan OB/GYN for her annual routine examination without a referral, and treatment for mental health conditions and substance abuse may be obtained by calling a specified facility directly.

This Plan has an option that allows a member to receive services outside of the standard HMO network. Read this brochure carefully to get a clear understanding of the benefits available through the self-referral program.

2. Choosing Your Doctor

The Plan's provider directory lists medical centers and doctors with their locations and phone numbers, and notes whether or not the doctor is accepting new patients. Directories are updated on a regular basis and are available at the time of enrollment or upon request by calling the Plan's Customer Relations Department. If you are interested in receiving care from a specific provider who is listed in the directory, call the provider to verify that he or she still participates with the Plan and is accepting new patients. Important note: When you enroll in this plans, services (except for emergency services) are provided through the Plan's delivery system; the continued availability and/or participation of any one doctor, hospital, or other provider, cannot be guaranteed.

When you enroll, you will be asked to complete a form and send it directly to the Plan, indicating the name of the medical center you are selecting for you and each member of your family. You also will be asked to indicate the name of the Primary Care Physician that you are selecting for you and each member of your family.

If you are receiving services from a doctor who leaves the Plan, the Plan will pay for covered services until the Plan can arrange with you for you to be seen by another participating doctor.

3. Referrals for Specialty Care

Except in a Medical Emergency, or when a Primary Care Doctor has designated another doctor to see patients, you must contact your Primary Care Doctor for a referral before seeing any other doctor or obtaining special services. Referral to a participating specialist is given at the Primary Care Doctor's discretion; if specialists or consultants are required beyond those participating in the Plan, the Primary Care Doctor will make arrangements for appropriate referrals.

When you receive a referral from your Primary Care Doctor, you must return to the Primary Care Doctor after the consultation unless your doctor authorizes additional visits. All follow-up care must be provided or arranged by the Primary Care Doctor. On referrals, the Primary Care Doctor will give specific instructions to the consultant as to when services are authorized. If additional services or visits are suggested by the consultant, you must first check with your Primary Care Doctor. Do not go to the specialist unless your Primary Care Doctor has arranged for and the Plan has issued an authorization for the referral in advance.

If you have a chronic or serious medical condition that causes you to see a Plan specialist frequently, your Primary Care Doctor will develop a treatment plan with you and your health plans that allows an adequate number of direct-access visits with that specialist. The treatment plan will permit you to visit your specialist without the need to obtain further referrals.

4. Authorizations

The Plan will provide benefits for Covered Services only when the services are medically necessary to prevent, diagnose, or treat your illness or condition. Your Primary Care Doctor must obtain the Plan's determination of medical necessity before you may be hospitalized, referred for speciality care, or obtain follow-up care from a specialist.

If you are a new Member who is already under the care of a specialist who is a Plan participant, you must still obtain a referral from a Plan Primary Care Doctor for the care to be covered by the Plan. If the doctor who originally referred you to this specialist is not your Plan Primary Care Doctor, you need only call to explain that you are now a Plan Member and ask that you be referred for your next appointment.

If you are selecting a new Primary Care Doctor and want to continue with this specialist, you must schedule an appointment so the Primary Care Doctor can decide whether to treat the condition directly or refer you back to the specialist.

If you require hospitalization, your Primary Care Doctor or authorized specialist will make the necessary arrangements and continue to supervise your care.

5. Out-of-Pocket Maximum

In addition to your share of the premiums, your out-of-pocket expenses for benefits covered under this Plan and authorized by Plan providers are limited to the state Co-payments that are required for a few benefits.

Section IV: What to Do If You Have Questions or Problems

1. Grievance Procedure

If we deny services or won't pay your claim, you may ask us to reconsider our decision. There are four basic elements to this procedure.

A. You may file a complaint by contacting a Customer Service Representative. The Customer Service Representative will investigate and attempt to resolve your complaint. Within fifteen days of receipt of your complaint, you will be notified of our position.

B. If you remain dissatisfied, you may file a written grievance with our Grievance Department. Your filing should refer to specific brochure wording explaining why you believe our decision is wrong. It must be made within six months from the date of the initial denial or refusal, except in extraordinary circumstances. Within fifteen days of receipt of your filing, the Grievance Department will provide you with a written response that either: (i) maintains the denial or refusal; (ii) pays the claim; (iii) arranges for the health care provider to give you the services; or (iv) requests further information.

C. If you are still dissatisfied, you may refile your written grievance with the Grievance Appeals Committee. The grievance must be filed within thirty business days of the notice of the Grievance Department's decision. The Grievance Appeals Committee is a committee of our employees appointed for the express purpose of reviewing and resolving grievances. Within fifteen days of receipt of the grievance, the Grievance Appeals Committee will render its decision in writing, consistent with the four subsections set forth in Section IV.1.B.

D. If you disagree with the ruling of the Grievance Appeals Committee, you may, within thirty business days, appeal to the Board of Directors. The appeal must be made in writing. The appeal will be reviewed by a committee appointed by the Board of Directors for the purpose of considering such appeals. You have the right to appear before the committee to present your case. The hearing will be scheduled not less than ten business days, nor more than fifteen business days, after the Board of Directors' receipt of the appeal, and will be held at the corporate office most convenient for you. The committee will issue a final ruling within fifteen business days of receipt of the appeal.

The ruling of the committee will be our final position.

2. Expedited Grievance Procedure

Occasionally medical circumstances require that certain procedures be performed without significant delay. These circumstances involve serious or life-threatening conditions, which are ones that may cause permanent loss of bodily functions or death if they are not treated as soon as possible. Upon request, denial of Precertification for such procedures will be given expedited review. If you believe that your circumstances require expedited review, you must so state in your initial written grievance to the Grievance Department. If the Grievance Department determines that there are no grounds for an expedited appeal, you will be notified immediately and the appeal will proceed on the time frame set forth in Section IV.1.

If the request for expedited review is appropriate, your expedited appeal will be reviewed within ten days by a committee appointed by the Board of Directors, as set forth in Section IV.1.D.

The committee will issue a final ruling within five business days of receipt of the appeal.

The ruling of the committee will be our final position.

3. Arbitration of Claims

Any claim for damages for personal injury, mental disturbance, or wrongful death arising out of the rendition or failure to render services under this contract must be submitted to binding arbitration.

Section V: Benefits

1. Medical and Surgical Benefits

A. WHAT IS COVERED

A comprehensive range of preventive, diagnostic and treatment services is provided by Plan doctors and other Plan providers. This includes all necessary office visits; you pay a $5 office visit co-pay, but no additional co-pay for laboratory tests, X rays and prenatal office visits. You pay nothing for well-child care for children under five years of age. Within the service area, house calls will be provided if in the judgment of the Plan doctor such care is necessary and appropriate; you pay nothing for a doctor's house call, or home visits by nurses and health aides.

The following services are included and are subject to the office visit co-pay unless stated otherwise.

- Preventive care, including well-baby care and periodic check-ups (co-pay waived for well-child care for children under age five)

- Vision and hearing screening when performed by a Plan Primary Care Doctor; complete hearing exam only when referred by a Plan Primary Care Doctor

- Mammograms are covered as follows: for woman age thirty-five through age thirty-nine, one mammogram during these five years; for women age forty through forty-nine, one mammogram every one or two years; for women age fifty through

213

sixty-four, one mammogram every year; and for women age sixty-five and above, one mammogram every two years. In addition to routine screening, mammograms are covered when prescribed by the doctor as Medically Necessary to diagnose or treat your illness

- Routine immunizations and boosters

- Consultations by specialists

- Complete obstetrical (maternity) care for all covered females, including prenatal, delivery, and postnatal care by a Plan doctor. Co-pays are waived for maternity care. The mother, at her option, may remain in the hospital up to forty-eight hours after a regular delivery and ninety-six hours after a cesarean delivery. Inpatient stays will be extended if medically necessary. If enrollment in the Plan is terminated during pregnancy, benefits will not be provided after coverage under the Plan has ended. Ordinary nursery care of the newborn child, when provided by a Plan doctor during the covered portion of the mother's hospital conferment for maternity, will be covered under either an individual or a family enrollment; other care of an infant who requires definitive treatment will be covered only if the infant is covered under a family enrollment.

- Voluntary sterilization and family planning services

- Diagnosis and treatment of diseases of the eye

- Allergy testing and treatment, including testing and treatment materials (such as allergy serum). You pay nothing.

- The insertion of internal prosthetic devices, such as pacemakers and artificial joints.

- Cornea, heart, heart-lung, kidney, liver, lung (single and double), pancreas and pancreas-kidney transplants; allogeneic (donor) bone-marrow transplants; autologous bone-marrow transplants (autologous stem-cell and peripheral stem-cell support) for the following conditions: acute lymphocytic or nonlymphocytic leukemia, advanced Hodgkin's lymphoma, advanced non-Hodgkin's lymphoma, advanced neuroblastoma, breast cancer, multiple myeloma, epithelial ovarian cancer, and testicular, mediastinal, retroperitoneal, and ovarian germ-cell tumors. Transplants are covered when approved by the Plan Medical Director. Related medical and hospital expenses of the donor are covered when the recipient is covered by this Plan.

- Women who undergo mastectomies may, at their option, have this procedure performed on an inpatient basis and remain in the hospital up to forty-eight hours after the procedure.

- Dialysis; you pay nothing.

- Chemotherapy and radiation therapy; you pay nothing

- Inhalation therapy

- Surgical treatment of morbid obesity

- Orthopedic devices, such as braces; foot orthotics, including replacement or adjustment limited to that necessitated by the Member's physical changes or growth

- Prosthetic devices, such as artificial limbs and lenses following cataract removal, including replacement or adjustment limited to that necessitated by the Member's physical changes or growth

- Durable medical equipment, such as wheelchairs, hospital beds, glucometers, and oxygen for home use, including equipment; you pay nothing

- Home health services by nurses and home health aides, including intravenous fluids and medications, when prescribed by your Plan doctor, who will periodically review the program for continuing appropriateness and need; you pay nothing

- All necessary medical or surgical care in a hospital or extended-care facility from Plan doctors and other Plan providers.

B. LIMITED BENEFITS

Oral and maxillofacial surgery is provided for nondental surgical and hospitalization procedures for congenital defects and for medical or surgical procedures occurring within or adjacent to the oral cavity or sinuses, including, but not limited to, treatment of fractures and excision of tumors and cysts. All other procedures involving the teeth or intraoral areas surrounding the teeth are not covered, including shortening of the mandible or maxillae for cosmetic purposes, correction of malocclusion, and any dental care involved in treatment of temporomandibular joint (TMJ) pain, except as defined previously.

Cleft lip and cleft palate benefits are provided for inpatient or outpatient expenses arising from: orthodontics; oral surgery; otologic, audiological, and speech/language treatment involved in one or both. You pay a $5 per office visit co-pay.

Reconstructive surgery will be provided to correct a condition resulting from a functional defect or from an injury or surgery that has produced a major effect on the Member's appearance and if the condition can reasonably be expected to be corrected by such surgery.

Short-term rehabilitative therapy (physical, speech, and occupational) is provided on an inpatient basis for up to two months per condition if significant improvement can be expected within two months; you pay nothing per session. Short-term rehabilitative therapy is provided on an outpatient basis; a combined benefit maximum for physical and occupational therapy is ninety visits per condition, per contract year; you pay $5 per visit. Speech therapy is covered for ninety visits, per condition, per contract year; you pay $5 per visit. Speech therapy is limited to treatment of certain speech impairments of organic origin. Occupational therapy is limited to services that assist the Member to achieve and maintain self-care and improved functioning in other activities of daily living. Plan benefits are only available to the extent that the plan provider determines they can be expected to result in the improvement of a member's condition.

Diagnosis and treatment of infertility is covered. You pay $5 per office visit. The following type of artificial insemination is covered: Intracervical insemination (ICI); you pay $5 per visit. Cost of donor sperm is not covered. Fertility drugs are not covered. Other assisted reproductive technology (ART) procedures such as in vitro fertilization, embryo transfer, and intrauterine insemination (IUI) are not covered.

C. WHAT IS NOT COVERED

- Physical examinations that are not necessary for medical reasons, such as those required for obtaining or continuing employment or insurance, attending school or camp, or travel

- Dental implants

- Reversal of voluntary, surgically induced sterility

- Surgery primarily for cosmetic purposes

- Homemaker services

- Hearing aids

- Transplants not listed as covered

- Long-term rehabilitative therapy

- Cardiac rehabilitation

- Chiropractic services

- Organ-donor-related transportation expenses

- Acupuncture services

- Blood and blood products

- Treatment of obesity and weight reduction programs (except for surgery for morbid obesity)

- Radial keratotomy and similar surgical procedures to correct retractive error

2. Hospital/Extended Care Benefits

A. WHAT IS COVERED

The Plan provides a comprehensive range of benefits with no dollar or day limit when you are hospitalized under the care of a Plan doctor. You pay nothing. All necessary services are covered, including:

- Semiprivate room accommodations; when a Plan doctor determines it is medically necessary, the doctor may prescribe private accommodations or private duty nursing care

- Specialized care units, such as intensive care or cardiac care units

- Blood and blood derivatives

The Plan provides a comprehensive range of benefits for up to one hundred days each calendar year when full-time skilled nursing care is necessary and confinement in a skilled nursing facility is medically appropriate as determined by a Plan doctor and approved by the Plan. You pay nothing. All necessary services are covered, including:

- Bed, board, and general nursing care

- Drugs, biologicals, supplies, and equipment ordinarily provided or arranged by the skilled nursing facility when prescribed by a Plan doctor.

- Supportive and palliative care for a terminally ill member is covered in the home or hospice facility. Services include inpatient and outpatient care and family counseling; these services are provided under the direction of a Plan doctor who certifies that the patient is in the terminal stage of illness, with a life expectancy of approximately six months or less

- Benefits are provided for ambulance transportation ordered or authorized by a Plan doctor

B. LIMITED BENEFITS

Hospitalization for certain dental procedures is covered when a Plan doctor determines there is a need for hospitalization for reasons totally unrelated to the dental procedure; the Plan will cover the hospitalization, but not the cost of the professional dental services. Conditions for which hospitalization would be covered include hemophilia and heart disease; the need for anesthesia, by itself, is not such a condition.

Hospitalization for medical treatment of substance abuse is limited to emergency care, diagnosis, treatment of medical conditions, and medical management of withdrawal symptoms (acute detoxification) if the Plan doctor determines that outpatient treatment is not medically appropriate.

C. WHAT IS NOT COVERED

- Personal comfort items, such as telephone and television

- Custodial care, rest cures, domiciliary or convalescent care

3. Emergency Benefits

A. WHAT IS A MEDICAL EMERGENCY?

A Medical Emergency is the sudden and unexpected onset of a condition or an injury that you believe endangers your life or could result in serious injury or disability, and requires immediate medical or surgical care. Some problems are emergencies because, if not treated promptly, they might become potentially life-threatening, such as heart attacks, strokes, poisonings, gunshot wounds, or the sudden inability to breathe. There are many other acute conditions that the Plan may determine are Medical Emergencies—what they all have in common is the need for quick action.

B. EMERGENCIES WITHIN THE SERVICE AREA

If you are in an emergency situation, please call your primary care doctor. In extreme emergencies, if you are unable to contact your doctor, contact the local emergency system (e.g., the 911 telephone system) or go to the nearest Hospital emergency room. Be sure to tell the emergency room personnel that you are a Plan member so they can notify the Plan. You or a family member should notify the Plan within forty-eight hours. It is your responsibility to ensure that the Plan has been timely notified.

If you need to be hospitalized, the Plan must be notified within forty-eight hours or on the first working day following your admission, unless it was not reasonably possible to notify the Plan within that time. If you are hospitalized in non-Plan facilities and Plan doctors believe care can be better provided in a Plan Hospital, you will be transferred when medically feasible with any ambulance charges covered in full.

Benefits are available for care from non-Plan providers in a medical emergency only if delay in reaching a Plan provider would result in death, disability, or significant jeopardy to your condition.

To be covered by this Plan, any follow-up care recommended by non-Plan providers must be approved by the Plan or provided by Plan providers, except as covered under POS benefits.

The Plan pays reasonable charges for emergency services to the extent the services would have been covered if received from Plan providers. You pay $25 per hospital emergency services to the extent the services would have been covered if received from Plan providers. If the emergency results in admission to a Hospital, the co-pay is waived.

C. EMERGENCIES OUTSIDE THE SERVICE AREA

Benefits are available for any medically necessary health service that is immediately required because of injury or unforeseen illness.

If you need to be hospitalized, the Plan must be notified within forty-eight hours or the first working day following your admission, unless it was not reasonably possible to notify the Plan within that time. If a Plan doctor believes care can be better provided in a Plan Hospital, you will be transferred when medically feasible with any ambulance charges covered in full.

To be covered by this Plan, any follow-up care recommended by non-Plan providers must be approved by the Plan or provided by Plan providers, except as covered under POS benefits.

The Plan pays reasonable charges for emergency services to the extent the services would have been covered if received from Plan providers. You pay $25 per Hospital emergency room or urgent care center visit for emergency services that are covered benefits of this Plan. If the emergency results in admission to a Hospital, the co-pay is waived.

D. WHAT IS COVERED

- Emergency care at a doctor's office or an urgent care center

- Emergency care as an outpatient or inpatient at a Hospital, including doctors' services

- Ambulance service approved by the Plan

With your authorization, the Plan will pay benefits directly to the providers of your emergency care upon receipt of their claims. Physician claims should be submitted on the HCFA 1500 claim form. If you are required to pay for the services, submit itemized bills and your receipts to the Plan along with an explanation of the services and the identification information from your ID card. Payment will be sent to you (or the provider, if you did not pay the bill), unless the claim is denied. If it is denied, you will receive notice of the decision, including the reasons for the denial and the provisions for the contract on which the denial was based. If you disagree with the Plan's decision, you may request reconsideration in accordance with the grievance procedure described in Section III.

E. WHAT IS NOT COVERED

- Elective care or nonemergency care, except as covered under POS benefits

- Emergency care provided outside the service area if the need for care could have been foreseen before leaving the service area, except as covered under POS benefits

- Medical and Hospital costs resulting from a normal full-term delivery of a baby outside the service area, except as covered under POS benefits

4. Mental Conditions/Substance-Abuse Benefits

A. WHAT IS COVERED

Treatment for mental health conditions and substance abuse may be obtained by calling our designated mental health facility. This facility will determine all appropriate referrals to specialists and facilities.

To the extent shown below, this Plan provides the following medically necessary services for the diagnosis and treatment of mental illness, or emotional disorder, drug abuse, and alcohol abuse. This Plan provides medical and Hospital services such as acute detoxification for the medical nonpsychiatric aspects of drug abuse and alcohol abuse, under the same terms and conditions as for any other illness or condition. Outpatient visits to Plan mental health providers for follow-up care are covered, as well as inpatient services necessary for diagnosis and treatment.

We also cover the following:

- Diagnostic evaluation

- Psychological testing

- Psychiatric, drug abuse, and alcohol abuse treatment (including individual and group therapy)

- Hospitalization (including inpatient professional services)

- Unlimited outpatient visits to Plan doctors, consultants, or other psychiatric personnel each calendar year; you pay $15 per visit for visits one through five; $25 per visit for visits six through thirty; $35 per visit thereafter for the remainder of the calendar year

- Up to 365 days of hospitalization for inpatient care each calendar year; you pay nothing

- Up to sixty days each calendar year for partial hospitalization; you pay a $5 co-pay per visit

B. WHAT IS NOT COVERED

- Care of psychiatric, drug abuse, and alcohol abuse conditions that in the professional judgment of Plan doctors are not treatable

- Psychiatric, drug abuse, and alcohol abuse evaluations or therapy on court order, or as a condition of parole or probation, unless determined by a Plan doctor to be necessary and appropriate

- Psychological testing that is not medically necessary to determine the appropriate treatment of a condition

- Treatment that is not authorized by a Plan doctor

5. Prescription Drug Benefits

A. WHAT IS COVERED

Prescription drugs prescribed by a Plan or referral doctor and obtained at a Plan pharmacy will be dispensed for up to a thirty-four-day supply; you pay a $5 co-pay per prescription unit or refill. Substitution of generic equivalents for name brand drugs will be made by Plan pharmacies, except when there is no generic equivalent of a name-brand drug or when an equivalent is available but a Plan doctor specifies only a name brand is to be used.

You may be required to use pharmacies associated with your medical center. Call your center or Primary Care Physician to determine which pharmacy must be used to fill your prescription. Covered medications and accessories include:

- Drugs for which a prescription is required by law

- Dental prescriptions when written by a Plan dentist

- Oral and injectable contraceptive drugs; contraceptive diaphragms and devices

- Implanted contraceptive drugs, such as Norplant

- Insulin

- Disposable needles and syringes needed for injecting covered prescribed medication

- Intravenous fluids and medications for home use are covered under Medical and Surgical benefits

- Diabetic supplies, including acetone test, alcohol swabs, blood-glucose control reagents, blood-glucose test kit, glucose-monitoring test supplies, insulin injection device, lancets, swabs, and test strips; you pay nothing

B. WHAT IS NOT COVERED

- Drugs available without a prescription or for which there is a nonprescription equivalent available

- Drugs obtained at a non-Plan pharmacy except for out-of-area emergencies

- Medical supplies such as dressings and antiseptics

- Vitamins and nutritional substances that can be purchased without a prescription

- Drugs for cosmetic purposes

- Drugs to enhance athletic performance

- Smoking-cessation drugs and medication, including nicotine patches

- Fertility drugs

Section VI: General Exclusions

The exclusions in this section apply to all benefits. Although we may list a specific service as a benefit, we will not cover it unless your Plan doctor determines it is medically necessary to prevent, diagnose, or treat your illness or condition. We do not cover the following:

- Care by non-Plan doctors or hospitals except for authorized referrals or emergencies (see Emergency Benefits) or eligible self-referral services obtained under Point-of-Service Benefits

- Expenses incurred while not covered by this Plan

- Services, drugs, or supplies that are not medically necessary

- Services that are not required according to accepted standards of medical, dental, or psychiatric practice

- Procedures, treatments, drugs, or devices that are experimental or investigational

- Procedures, services, drugs, and supplies related to sex transformations

- Procedures, services, drugs, and supplies related to abortions except when the life of the mother would be endangered if the fetus were carried to term or when the pregnancy is the result of an act of rape or incest

Section VII: General Limitations

1. Important Notice

Although a specific service may be listed as a benefit, it will be covered for you only if, in the judgment of your Plan doctor, it is medically necessary for the prevention, diagnosis, or treatment of your illness or condition. No oral statement of any person shall modify or otherwise affect the benefits, limitations, and exclusions of this brochure, convey or void any coverage, increase or reduce any benefits under this Plan, or be used in the prosecution or defense of a claim under this Plan. This brochure is the official statement of benefits on which you rely.

2. Medicare

Tell us if you or a family member is enrolled in Medicare Part A or B. Medicare will determine who is responsible for paying for medical services and we will coordinate the payments. On occasion, you may need to file a Medicare claim form.

3. Double Coverage

When anyone has coverage with us and with another group health plan, it is called double coverage. You must tell us if you or a family member has double coverage. You must also send us documents about other insurance if we ask for them.

When you have double coverage, one plan is the primary payer; it pays benefits first. The other plan is secondary; it pays benefits next. We decide which insurance is primary according to the National Association of Insurance Commissioners' Guidelines.

If we pay second, we determine what the reasonable charge for the benefit should be. After the first plan pays, we will pay either what is left of the reasonable charge or our regular benefit, whichever is less. We will not pay more than the reasonable charge. If we are the secondary payer, we may be entitled to receive payment from your primary plan.

We will always provide you with the benefits described in this brochure. Remember: even if you do not file a claim with your other plan, you must still tell us that you have double coverage.

4. Extraordinary Circumstances

Under certain extraordinary circumstances, we may have to delay your services or be unable to provide them. In that case, we will make all reasonable efforts to provide you with necessary care.

5. Your Reimbursement Obligations

When you receive money to compensate you for medical or hospital care for injuries or illness that another person caused, you must reimburse us for whatever services we paid for. We will cover the costs of treatment that exceeds the amount you received in the settlement. If you do not seek damages, you must agree to let us try. This is called subrogation. If you need more information, contact us for our subrogation procedures.

6. Workers' Compensation

We do not cover services that you need because of a workplace-related disease or injury. Once you have received the maximum workers' compensation benefits, we will provide your benefits.

Section VIII: Point-of-Service Benefits

1. Facts About the Point-of-Service Benefits

At your option, you may choose to obtain benefits covered by this Plan from non-Plan doctors and Hospitals whenever you need care, except for the benefits listed below under "What Is Not Eligible for Self-Referral." Benefits not covered under Point-of-Service benefits must either be received from or arranged by Plan doctors to be covered. When you obtain covered nonemergency medical treatment form a non-Plan doctor without a referral from a Plan doctor, you are subject to the deductibles, coinsurance, and maximum benefits stated below.

Members may self-refer for most services. Some services, shown below, must be referred by your Primary Care Physician. For eligible self-referral services, the Plan pays 80 percent of the allowable benefits after you pay a $200 calendar year deductible for an individual, or $400 for a family. Expenses incurred in the last month of the calendar year, which are used to satisfy the deductible, will apply to the deductible of the following calendar year. You pay the deductible and 20 percent of the allowed benefit. If the actual charge for a covered service is more than the allowed benefit, you must also pay the difference.

Preauthorization from the Plan is required for certain services, as shown below, when not of an emergency nature. You or your physician must call the Plan for authorization. If you do not call for authorization, you risk having to pay 40 percent of the allowed benefits after the deductible and take the chance that the procedure is not a covered benefit.

This self-referral program has an out-of-pocket maximum based on deductible and coinsurance payments. Once out-of-pocket expenses for deductibles and coinsurance reach $2,000 per member or $4,000 per family, the Plan will pay 100 percent of the allowed benefit for the reminder of the calendar year. Coinsurance amounts for failure to obtain preauthorization do not contribute toward the out-of-pocket maximum.

Although self-referral benefits are available for some services, you should remember that the out-of-pocket costs are lower through the standard HMO benefit.

An allowed benefit is the acceptable charge the Plan uses to calculate the reimbursement to a health care provider that is not under contract with the Plan. The Member is responsible for any amount that exceeds the allowed benefit determined by the Plan, plus the stated coinsurance payment.

Benefits under the self-referral program are subject to the definition, limitations, and exclusions shown elsewhere in this Plan. The Plan determines the medical necessity of services and supplies provided to prevent, diagnose, or treat an illness or condition.

2. Medical and Surgical Benefits

At your option, you can choose to self-refer for the following services instead of getting a referral from your Primary Care Physician. You pay 20 percent of the allowed benefit after the deductible.

- Physician office, home, or hospital visits

- Specialist care and consultation

- Allergy testing and treatment

- Maternity, annual Pap smears, and pelvic exams

- Diagnostic laboratory and X-ray tests

- Surgical procedures (preauthorization required)

- Periodic physical exams, immunizations, and well-child care

- Physical, speech, or occupational therapy

- Home health care (preauthorization required)

- Durable medical equipment, prosthetics, and orthopedic devices (preauthorization required)

- Hearing and visions exams

- Family planning and sterilizations

- Dialysis, chemotherapy, radiation therapy, and inhalation therapy

- Infertility services (preauthorization required)

The following services must be provided by or referred to specialists by your Primary Care Physician or the Plan. You cannot self-refer for the following services:

- Health education services

- Dental care benefits

- Emergency and urgent care benefits.

3. Hospital/Extended-Care Benefits

You can choose to be admitted for an inpatient Hospital stay through self-referral. You must notify the Plan in advance of any self-referral admission and the admission must be preauthorized by the Plan. You pay 20 percent and any charges over the allowed benefit after the $200 deductible is satisfied. If preauthorization is not obtained, you pay 40 percent of the allowed benefit after the deductible. To obtain preauthorization, call the Plan. In addition to the services noted above, the following require preauthorization:

- Inpatient hospitalization

- Skilled nursing facility

- Hospice care

4. Mental Conditions/Substance-Abuse Benefits

You can choose to self-refer for inpatient Hospital and outpatient care. You must call the Plan to obtain a preauthorization prior to receiving any self-referral services. You pay 20 percent and any charges above the allowed benefit after the deductible is satisfied for all covered services except outpatient care. Outpatient care will be covered after the deductible. You pay 20 percent of the allowed benefit and any charges above the allowed benefit per visit for visits one through five; you pay 35 percent of the allowed benefits and any charges above the allowed benefit per visit for visits six through thirty; you pay 50 percent of the allowed benefit and any charges above the allowed benefit per visit thereafter for the remainder of the calendar year.

If preauthorization is not obtained for inpatient care, you pay 40 percent of the allowed charges after the deductible. To obtain preauthorization or inpatient or outpatient care, call the Plan.

5. Emergency Care

Emergency services will be treated as a standard HMO benefit and only provided through the HMO delivery system. Please refer to the section in this Plan covering emergency benefits.

6. Other Covered Benefits

Prescriptions written as a result of a self-referral to a doctor are eligible for a $5 Co-payment for a thirty-four-day supply as long as they are filled at a Plan participating pharmacy. If a non-participating pharmacy is used, you pay 20 percent of the allowed benefit after the deductible, and any costs in excess of the allowed benefit.

7. How To File Claims

Call the Customer Services Department for claim forms and submit your claims in accordance with their instructions.

Section IX: Definitions

Defined terms will appear capitalized throughout the Agreement.

Acute: The sudden onset of disease or injury, or a sudden change in the Member's condition that would require prompt medical attention.

Agreement: The Enrollment Agreement between you and us, including any riders, attachments, and certificates.

Ambulatory Surgical Centers: A facility currently licensed by the appropriate state regulatory agency for the provision of surgical and related medical services on an outpatient basis.

Certificate: The certificate of insurance issued to you by us.

Coinsurance: The percentage of the cost of the covered services you pay toward your submitted claims once you have met your deductible. The Coinsurances applicable to your Plan are listed in your Summary of Benefits.

Congenital Anomaly: A condition existing at or from birth that is a significant deviation from the common form or norm. For purposes of this Plan, Congenital Anomalies include protruding ear deformities, cleft lips, cleft palates, birthmarks, webbed fingers or toes, and other conditions that the Carrier may determine to be Congenital Anomalies. In no event will the term Congenital Anomaly include conditions relating to teeth or interoral structures.

Contract Year: The twelve-month period commencing on the effective date of the Agreement or any anniversary date thereafter, during which the Agreement is in effect.

Co-payment: The amount you are required to pay directly to a Network Provider at the time Covered services are rendered.

Cover, Covered, or Covered Services: The Medically Necessary services paid for or arranged for you by us under the terms and conditions of this Certificate.

Covered Dependents: Dependents, as defined in the Certificate, who are Members.

Dependents: Your spouse, unmarried and newborn children as described in the Certificate.

Enrollment Form: Our form, which Member must complete to enroll in the Plan.

Experimental or Investigational: A drug, device, or biological product is Experimental or Investigational if the drug, device, or biological product cannot be lawfully marketed without approval of the U.S. Food and Drug Administration (FDA) and approval for marketing has not been given at the time it is furnished. Approval means all forms of acceptance by the FDA.

A medical treatment or procedure, or a drug, device, or biological product is Experimental or Investigational if (1) reliable evidence shows that it is the subject of ongoing phase I, II, or III clinical trials or under study to determine its maximum tolerated dose, its toxicity, its safety, its efficacy, or its efficacy as compared with the standard means of treatment or diagnosis; or (2) reliable evidence shows that the consensus among experts regarding the drug, device, or biological product or medical treatment or procedure is that further studies or clinical trials are necessary to determine its maximum tolerated dose, its toxicity, its safety, its efficacy, or its efficacy as compared with the standard means of treatment or diagnosis.

Reliable evidence shall mean only published reports and articles in the authoritative medical and scientific literature; the written protocol or protocols used by the treating facility or the protocol(s) of another facility studying substantially the same drug, device, or medical treatment or procedure; or the written informed consent used by the treating facility or by another facility studying substantially the same drug, device, or medical treatment or procedure.

Determination of Experimental/Investigational status may require review of appropriate government publications such as those of the National Institutes of Health, National Cancer Institute, Agency for Health Care Policy and Research, Food and Drug Administration, and National Library of Medicine. Independent evaluation and opinion by Board Certified Physicians who are professors, associate professors, or assistant professors of medicine at recognized United States Medical Schools may be obtained for their expertise in subspecialty areas.

Home Health Care Agency: An organization currently certified or licensed by the state to render home health care services

Hospital: An institution rendering inpatient and outpatient services for the medical care of the sick or injured. It must be accredited as a Hospital by either the Joint Commission on Accreditation of Health Care Facilities or the Bureau of Hospitals of the American Osteopathic Association. A Hospital may be a general, acute-care, or a specialty institution, provided that it is appropriately accredited as such, and currently licensed by the proper state authorities.

Medical Emergency: The sudden and unexpected onset of a condition or an injury that you believe endangers your life or could result in serious injury or disability, and requires immediate medical or surgical care that the covered person secures within seventy-two hours after the onset. Medical Emergencies include deep cuts, broken bones, heart attacks, cardiovascular accidents, poisonings, loss of consciousness or respiration, convulsions, and such other acute conditions as may be determined by the Carrier to be Medical Emergencies.

Medically Necessary: Services, drugs, supplies, equipment provided by a hospital or covered provider of health care services that the Carrier determines: (1) are appropriate to diagnose or treat the patient's condition, illness, or injury; (2) are consistent with standards of good medical practice in the United States; (3) are not primarily for the personal comfort or convenience of the patient, the family, or the provider: (4) are not a part of or associated with the scholastic, educational, or vocational training of the patient; and (5) in the case of inpatient care, cannot be provided safely on an outpatient basis. The fact that a covered provider has prescribed, recommended, or approved a service, supply, drug, or equipment does not, in itself, make it Medically Necessary.

Medicare: Title XVIII of the Social Security Act, as amended.

Mental Conditions/Substance Abuse: Conditions and diseases listed in the most recent edition of the International Classification of Diseases (ICD) as psychoses, neurotic disorders, or personality disorders; other nonpsychotic mental disorders listed in the ICD to be determined by the Carrier; or disorders listed in the ICD requiring treatment for abuse of or dependence upon substances such as alcohol, narcotics, or hallucinogens.

Network Physician: A physician who, at the time of providing or referring Covered Services, was under contract with us to provide Covered Services to our Members.

Network Provider: A physician, Hospital, skilled nursing facility, Home Health Care Agency, or any other duly licensed or certified institution or health professional which, at the time of providing or referring Covered Services, was under contract with us to provide Covered Services to our Members.

Network Specialist: A Network Provider who has limited his or her practice to certain areas of medicine and who, at the time of providing or referring Covered Services, was under contract with us to provide Covered Services to our Members.

Physician: A currently licensed doctor of medicine or osteopathy.

Precertification: An authorization given by us that you must receive before you can obtain certain Covered Services. We indicate which Covered Services require Precertification in the Certificate. Covered Services obtained without a required Precertification will be Covered at a greater cost of you.

Preexisting Condition: A disease or a physical condition for which a Member, as an ordinary prudent person, should have sought treatment, diagnosis, or medical advice within six months immediately prior to becoming Covered under this Certificate; or treatment, diagnosis, or medical advice was actually recommended or received within six months immediately prior to becoming Covered under this Certificate. A pregnancy existing on the effective date of coverage is a Preexisting Condition.

Primary Care Physician: A Network Physician who, under the Certificate, provides initial care and basic medical services, initiates referrals for specialty care, and is listed in the roster of Network Providers as a Primary Care Physician.

Reasonable and Customary: Those charges that are comparable to charges made by other providers for similar services and supplies under comparable circumstances in the same geographic area.

Rehabilitation Facility: A currently licensed and accredited facility that primarily provides physical therapy treatment.

Skilled Nursing Facility: An institution or a distinct part of an institution that is licensed or approved under state or local law, primarily engaged in providing skilled nursing care and related services.

Specialized Rehabilitation Facility: A Hospital or other facility that is certified for the treatment of alcohol or drug-dependent individuals, respectively. It provides nursing, medical counseling, and therapeutic services to such individuals according to individualized treatment plans. Transitional living facilities are excluded from this definition.

Urgent Care: A licensed facility, except a Hospital, that provides urgent care.

CONTACT LIST FOR STATE INSURANCE COMMISSIONERS

ALABAMA
Commissioner of Insurance
P.O. Box 303351
Montgomery, AL 36130-3351
334-241-9903

ALASKA
Director of Insurance
P.O. Box 110805
Juneau, AK 99811-0805
907-465-2515

ARIZONA
Director of Insurance
2910 North 44th Street,
Suite 210
Phoenix, AZ 85018
602-912-8400

ARKANSAS
Insurance Commissioner
1200 West 3rd Street
Little Rock, AR 72201
800-852-5494

CALIFORNIA
Commissioner of Insurance
300 Capitol Mall, Suite 1600
Sacramento, CA 95814
916-445-5544 or 800-927-
HELP

COLORADO
Commissioner of Insurance
1560 Broadway, Suite 850
Denver, CO 80202
303-894-7499

CONNECTICUT
Insurance Commissioner
P.O. Box 816
Hartford, CT 06142-0816
860-297-3800

DELAWARE
Insurance Commissioner
The Rodney Building
841 Silver Lake Boulevard
Dover, DE 19904
302-739-4251 or 800-282-8611

DISTRICT OF COLUMBIA
Superintendent of Insurance
810 First St., N.E.
Suite 701
Washington, D.C. 20002
202-727-8000 or 202-727-7434

FLORIDA
Insurance Commissioner
200 East Gaines St.
Tallahassee, FL 32399-0300
850-922-3100

GEORGIA
Insurance Commissioner
2 Martin Luther King Jr. Drive
16 West Tower
Atlanta, GA 30334
404-656-2070

HAWAII
Insurance Commissioner
P.O. Box 3614
Honolulu, HI 96811
808-586-2790

IDAHO
Director of Insurance
P.O. Box 83720
Boise, ID 83720
208-334-2250

ILLINOIS
Director of Insurance
320 West Washington Street,
Fourth Floor
Springfield, IL 62767
217-782-4515 or 217-782-7446

INDIANA
Commissioner of Insurance
311 West Washington Street,
Suite 300
Indianapolis, IN 46204
317-232-2385 or 800-622-4461

IOWA
Commissioner of Insurance
330 Maple St.
Des Moines, IA 50319
515-281-5705

KANSAS
Commissioner of Insurance
420 South West Ninth Street
Topeka, KS 66612
800-432-2484

KENTUCKY
Insurance Commissioner
P.O. Box 517
Frankfort, KY 40602
502-564-3630

LOUISIANA
Commissioner of Insurance
P.O. Box 94214

Baton Rouge, LA 70804
225-342-5900

MAINE
Superintendent of Insurance
State House
Station 34
Augusta, ME 04333
207-624-8511

MARYLAND
Insurance Commissioner
525 St. Paul Place
Baltimore, MD 21202
800-492-6116

MASSACHUSETTS
Commissioner of Insurance
One South Station, 5th Floor
Boston, MA 02110

MICHIGAN
Commissioner of Insurance
P.O. Box 30220
Lansing, MI 48909
517-373-9273

MINNESOTA
Commissioner of Commerce
133 East Seventh Street
St. Paul, MN 55101
651-296-2488

MISSISSIPPI
Commissioner of Insurance
1804 Walter Sillers Building
550 High Street
Jackson, MS 39201
601-359-3569 or 800-562-2957

MISSOURI
Director of Insurance

301 West High Street 6 North
P.O. Box 690
Jefferson City, MO 65102-0690
800-726-7390

MONTANA
Commissioner of Insurance
P.O. Box 4009
Helena, MT 59604
406-444-2040 or 800-332-6148

NEBRASKA
Director of Insurance
941 O Street, Suite 400
Lincoln, NE 68508
402-471-2201

NEVADA
Commissioner of Insurance
788 Fairview Drive, Suite 300
Carson City, NV 89701
775-687-4270

NEW HAMPSHIRE
Insurance Commissioner
56 Old Suncook Rd.
Concord, NH 03301
603-271-2261 or 800-852-3416

NEW JERSEY
Commissioner of Insurance
20 West State Street
Trenton, NJ 08625
609-292-5300

NEW MEXICO
Superintendent of Insurance
P.O. Drawer 1269
Santa Fe, NM 87504-1269
505-827-4601

NEW YORK
Superintendent of Insurance
25 Beaver Street
New York, NY 10004
212-480-6400

NORTH CAROLINA
Commissioner of Insurance
P.O. Box 26387
Raleigh, NC 27611
919-733-2032 or 800-662-7777

NORTH DAKOTA
Commissioner of Insurance
Capitol Building, Fifth Floor
600 East Boulevard
Bismarck, ND 58505-0320
800-247-0560

OHIO
Director of Insurance
2100 Stella Court
Columbus, OH 43215
614-644-2658 or 800-686-1526

OKLAHOMA
Insurance Commissioner
P.O. Box 53408
Oklahoma City, OK 73152-3408
405-521-2828

OREGON
Insurance Division
350 Winter Street NE, Rm 440
Salem, OR 97301
503-947-7980

PENNSYLVANIA
Insurance Commissioner

1326 Strawberry Square, 13th Floor
Harrisburg, PA 17120
717-787-5173

RHODE ISLAND
Associate Director and
Superintendent of Insurance
233 Richmond Street
Providence, RI 02903
401-222-2246

SOUTH CAROLINA
Chief Insurance Commissioner
P.O. Box 100105
Columbia, SC 29202-3105
803-737-6212

SOUTH DAKOTA
Director of Insurance
118 West Capitol
Pierre, SD 57501
605-773-3563

TENNESSEE
Commissioner of Insurance
500 James Robertson Parkway
Nashville, TN 37243-0565
615-741-2241 or 800-252-3439

TEXAS
Commissioner of Insurance
333 Guadalupe
P.O. Box 149091
Austin, TX 78714-9091
800-252-3439

UTAH
Commissioner of Insurance
Rm. 3110 State Office Building,

Salt Lake City, UT 84114
801-538-3800 or 800-439-3805

VERMONT
Commissioner of Banking,
Securities, and Insurance
State Office Building
89 Main St., Drawer 20
Montpelier, VT 05602-3101
802-828-3301

VIRGINIA
Commissioner of Insurance
P.O. Box 1157
Richmond, VA 23218
804-371-9741 or 800-552-7945

WASHINGTON
Insurance Commissioner
Insurance Building
P.O. Box 40256
Olympia, WA 98504

800-562-6900

WEST VIRGINIA
Insurance Commissioner
P.O. Box 50540
Charleston, WV 25305
304-558-3394 or 800-642-9004

WISCONSIN
Commissioner of Insurance
P.O. Box 7873
121 East Wilson Street
Madison, WI 53707
608-266-0103 or 800-236-8517

WYOMING
Insurance Commissioner
Herschler Building,
3rd Floor East
122 West 25th Street
Cheyenne, WY 82002
307-777-7401

CONTACT LIST FOR STATE ATTORNEYS GENERAL

ALABAMA
Office of the Attorney General
State House
11 South Union Street
Montgomery, AL 36130
334-242-7300

ALASKA
Office of the Attorney General
P.O. Box 110300
Diamond Courthouse
Juneau, AK 99811-0300
907-465-3600

ARIZONA
Office of the Attorney General
1275 West Washington Street
Phoenix, AZ 85007
602-542-4266

ARKANSAS
Office of the Attorney General
200 Tower Building
323 Center Street
Little Rock, AR 72201
501-682-2007

CALIFORNIA
Office of the Attorney General
1300 I Street, Suite 1740
Sacramento, CA 95814
916-324-5437

COLORADO
Office of the Attorney General
Department of Law

1525 Sherman Street,
7th Floor
Denver, CO 80203
303-866-4500

CONNECTICUT
Office of the Attorney General
55 Elm Street
Hartford, CT 06141-0120
860-808-5318

DELAWARE
Office of the Attorney General
Carvel State Office Building
820 North French Street
Wilmington, DE 19801
302-577-8400

DISTRICT OF COLUMBIA
Office of the Corporation
Counsel
441 Fourth Street N.W.
Washington, D.C. 20001
202-727-6248

FLORIDA
Office of the Attorney General
107 W. Gaines St.
Tallahassee, FL 32399-1050
850-487-1963

GEORGIA
Office of the Attorney General
40 Capitol Square, S.W.
Atlanta, GA 30334-1300
404-656-4585

HAWAII
Office of the Attorney General
425 Queen Street

Honolulu, HI 96813
808-586-1282

IDAHO
Office of the Attorney General
Statehouse
Boise, ID 83720-1000
208-334-2400

ILLINOIS
Office of the Attorney General
James R. Thompson Center
100 West Randolph Street
Chicago, IL 60601
312-814-2503

INDIANA
Office of the Attorney General
Indiana Government Center
South, Fifth floor
402 West Washington Street
Indianapolis, IN 46204
317-232-6201

IOWA
Office of the Attorney General
Hoover State Office Building
Des Moines, IA 50319
515-281-3053

KANSAS
Office of the Attorney General
Judicial Building
301 West Tenth Street
Topeka, KS 66612-1597
785-296-2215

KENTUCKY
Office of the Attorney General
State Capitol, Room 116

Frankfort, KY 40601
502-696-5300

Office of the Attorney General
Department of Justice
P.O. Box 94005
Baton Rouge, LA 70801
225-342-7013

MAINE
Office of the Attorney General
State House, Station Six
Augusta, ME 04333
207-626-8800

MARYLAND
Office of the Attorney General
200 St. Paul Place
Baltimore, MD 21202-2202
410-576-6300

MASSACHUSETTS
Office of the Attorney General
One Ashburton Place
Boston, MA 02108-1698
617-727-2200

MICHIGAN
Office of the Attorney General
P.O. Box 30212
525 West Ottawa Street
Lansing, MI 48909-0212
517-373-1110

MINNESOTA
Office of the Attorney General
State Capitol, Suite 102
St. Paul, MN 55155
651-296-6196

MISSISSIPPI
Office of the Attorney General
Department of Justice
P.O. Box 220
Jackson, MS 39205-0220
601-359-3680

MISSOURI
Office of the Attorney General
Supreme Court Building
207 West High Street
P.O. Box 899
Jefferson City, MO 65102
573-751-3321

MONTANA
Office of the Attorney General
Justice Building
215 North Sanders
Helena, MT 59620-1401
406-444-2026

NEBRASKA
Office of the Attorney General
2115 State Capitol
Lincoln, NE 68509
402-471-2682

NEVADA
Office of the Attorney General
Old Supreme Court Building
100 North Carson Street
Carson City, NV 89701
775-684-1100.

NEW HAMPSHIRE
Office of the Attorney General
33 Capitol Street
Concord, NH 03301
603-271-3658

NEW JERSEY
Office of the Attorney General
Department of Law and
Public Safety
P.O. Box 080
Trenton, NJ 08625
609-292-4925

NEW MEXICO
Office of the Attorney General
P.O. Drawer 1508
Santa Fe, NM 87504-1508
505-827-6000

NEW YORK
Office of the Attorney General
Department of Law
The Capitol, Second Floor
Albany, NY 12224
518-474-7330

NORTH CAROLINA
Office of the Attorney General
Department of Justice
P.O. Box 629
Raleigh, NC 27602-0629
919-716-6400

NORTH DAKOTA
Office of the Attorney General
State Capitol
600 East Boulevard Avenue,
Dept 125
Bismarck, ND 58505-0040
701-328-2210

OHIO
Office of the Attorney General
State Office Tower
30 East Broad Street,
17th Floor

Columbus, OH 43215-3428
614-466-4320

OKLAHOMA
Office of the Attorney General
State Capitol
2300 North Lincoln Boulevard,
Room 112
Oklahoma City, OK 73105
405-521-3921

OREGON
Office of the Attorney General
Justice Building
1162 Court Street, N.E.
Salem, OR 97310
503-378-6002

PENNSYLVANIA
Office of the Attorney General
Strawberry Square, 16th Floor
Harrisburg, PA 17120
717-787-5211

RHODE ISLAND
Office of the Attorney General
150 South Main Street
Providence, RI 02903
401-274-4400

SOUTH CAROLINA
Office of the Attorney General
Rembert C. Dennis Office
Building
P.O. Box 11549
Columbia, SC 29211-1549
803-734-3970

SOUTH DAKOTA
Office of the Attorney General
500 East Capitol

Pierre, SD 57501-5070
605-773-3215

TENNESSEE
Office of the Attorney General
425 5th Avenue
Nashville, TN 37243-0485
615-741-5860

TEXAS
Office of the Attorney General
Capitol Station
P.O. Box 12548
Austin, TX 78711-2548
512-463-2100

UTAH
Office of the Attorney General
State Capitol, Room 236
Salt Lake City, UT 84114-0810
801-538-1326

VERMONT
Office of the Attorney General
109 State Street
Montpelier, VT 05609-1001
802-828-3171

VIRGINIA
Office of the Attorney General

900 East Main Street
Richmond, VA 23219
804-786-2071

WASHINGTON
Office of the Attorney General
P.O. Box 40100
1125 Washington Street, S.E.
Olympia, WA 98504-0100
360-753-6200

WEST VIRGINIA
Office of the Attorney General
State Capitol
1900 Kanawha Boulevard East
Charleston, WV 25305
304-558-2021

WISCONSIN
Office of the Attorney General
State Capitol, P.O. Box 7857
Suite 114 East
Madison, WI 53707-7857
608-266-1221

WYOMING
Office of the Attorney General
123 Capitol Building
200 W. 29th Street
Cheyenne, WY 82002
307-777-7841

CONTACT LIST FOR SELECTED ORGANIZATIONS

The following is a list of: (a) various organizations that assist consumers with health care issues; (b) research organizations that study consumer-related issues; and (c) government organizations with regulatory and analytical functions. This list is not all-inclusive; apologies are offered to the many valuable and hard-working organizations that are not included here.

AARP
601 E Street., N.W.
Washington, D.C. 20049
202-434-2277
Web site: www.aarp.org

Alliance for Health Reform
1900 L Street, N.W.,
Suite 512
Washington, D.C. 20036
202-466-5626
Web site: www.allhealth.org

Center for Medicare
Advocacy, Inc.
P.O. Box 350
Willimantic, Ct. 06226
860-456-7790

Web site: www.medicare advo-
cacy.org

Center for Patient Advocacy
1350 Beverly Road, Suite 108
McLean, VA 22101
703-748-0400 or 800-846-7444
Web site:
www.patientadvocacy.org

Citizens' Council on Health
Care
1954 University Avenue West,
Suite 8
St. Paul, Minn. 55104
651-646-8935
Web site: www.cchc-mn.org

Community Catalyst
30 Winter Street
Boston, MA 02108
(617) 338-6035
Web site:
www.communitycat.org

Consumer Coalition for Quality Health Care
1101 Vermont Ave, N.W.,
Suite 1001
Washington, D.C. 20005
202-789-3606
Web site: www.consumers.org

Consumers for Affordable
Health Care
P.O. Box 2490
Augusta, Maine 04338-2490
207-622-7045
Web site: www.mainecahc.org

Consumers Union
101 Truman Avenue
Yonkers NY 10703
914-378-2000
Web sites:
www.consumersunion.org
www consumerreports.org

Families, USA
1334 G Street, N.W.
Washington, D.C. 20005
202-628-3030
Web site: www.familiesusa.org

Health Care for All
30 Winter Street, #1010
Boston, MA 02108
617-350-7279
Web site: www.hcfama.org

Kaiser Family Foundation
2400 Sand Hill Road
Menlo Park, CA 94025
650-854-9400 or 800-656-4533
Web site: www.kff.org

National Alliance for the Men-
tally Ill
Colonial Place Three
2107 Wilson Boulevard,
Suite 300
Arlington, Va. 22201-3042
703-524-7600 or 800-950-6264
Web site: www.nami.org

National Association of Insurance Commissioners
444 North Capitol Street,
Suite 701
Washington, D.C. 20001-1512

202-624-7790
Web site: www.naic.org

National Coalition on Health Care
1200 G Street, N.W.,
Suite 750
Washington, D.C. 20005
202-638-7151
Web site: www.nchc.org

National Conference of State Legislatures
444 North Capitol Street, N.W.
Washington, D.C. 20001
202-624-5400
Web site: www.ncsl.org

National Health Policy Forum
2021 K Street, N.W.,
Suite 800
Washington, D.C. 20052
202-872-1390
Web site: nhpf.org

National Mental Health Association
1021 Prince Street

Alexandria, Va. 22314-2971
703-684-7722
Web site: www.nmha.org

Patient Advocate Foundation
753 Thimble Shoals Boulevard, #B
Newport News, VA 23606
757-873-6668

Physicians Who Care
12125 Jones Maltsberger, Suite 607
San Antonio, TX 78247
210-545-5840
Web site: www.pwc.org

Public Citizen
1600 Twentieth St., N.W.
Washington, D.C. 20009
202-588-1000
Web site: www.citizen.org

Tennessee Health Care Campaign
1103 Chapel Avenue
Nashville, TN 37206
615-227-7500
Web site: www.thccz.org

If you'd like to get in touch with me, hopefully to share a success story, I can be reached at RDOrin@aol.com.